the Compass and the Nail

CRAIG WILSON

the Compass and the Nail

How the Patagonia model of loyalty can save your business, and might just save the planet

A GENUINE VIREO BOOK

VIREO/RARE BIRD

453 South Spring Street · Suite 302 · Los Angeles · CA 90013 · rarebirdbooks.com

FIRST TRADE PAPERBACK EDITION

Printed in the United States
Set in Tiempos

PAPERBACK ISBN: 9781947856615

Publisher's Cataloging-in-Publication data.
Wilson, Craig P.
The Compass and the Nail: How the Patagonia Model of Loyalty Can Save Your Business, and Might Just Save the Planet / by Craig Wilson. p. cm.
ISBN 9781942600060
Includes bibliographical references and index.
1. Patagonia, Inc. 2. Success in business. 3. Business enterprises—Environmental aspects. 4. Social responsibility of business. 5. Green products. 6. Management—Environmental aspects. I. Title.
HD9948.5.A2 .W55 2015
381/.45687—dc23

"A rusty nail placed near a faithful compass, will sway it from the truth, and wreck the argosy."

SIR WALTER SCOTT

Contents

1. Right Livelihood 1

2. Choosing to See 15

3. *Why* Matters: The Basis for Inspired Relationships 29

4. *How* Matters: The Brand Ecosystem 39

   The Science of Building Advocacy 47
   The Story Universe 54
   The Customer Activation Cycle 56
   Long-term Sustainable Loyalty
   Defined in Terms of Value 63
   The Progression of Resonance 65
   Light & Motion's Story Universe
   —The Visual 72

5. Exploring Purposeful Connection 77

6. Throwing the Baby Out with the Bath Water 101

7. Errors in Judgment 129

8. The Macro View 149

9. Grow Your Own Apple 173

10. Standing on the Edge of Some Crazy Cliff 205

11. Understanding Advocacy: Defined Terms 227

12. Index 231

13. Acknowledgments 243

**"You say you want
diamonds on a ring of gold."**

U2

CHAPTER ONE

Right Livelihood

As much as we've been told to believe businesses change the face of our society, economy, and quality of life, the reality is that consumers are the ones that truly create and propel change.

While Silicon Valley obsesses over the next big thing, the majority of businesses endeavor to serve their customers profitably and sustainably by competing in the trenches each and every workaday day. This is what turns the wheels of our global economy, everyday businesses competing for the attention of the everyday consumer. And so it goes. It's the consumer that decides who stays and who goes. It truly is a democratic system. The spoils go to the provider that meets the needs of the user most intimately. This book is meant to help just these businesses understand marketing as a means to invoke change, as a process that engenders fierce loyalty in customers, engaging them as lifelong advocates.

It's been posited that it's up to the leaders of business today to address the difficulties of the present day woes of the world by behaving more responsibly socially, environmentally, financially, and even ethically. That somehow, we the consuming public are lemmings without the wherewithal to fashion the changes required to make our world more inhabitable, more economically viable, more socially conscious, even more equitable.

The truth is, we—the buying public—choose the companies that serve us, and therefore defeat or propel their actions.

Unfortunately, we as an aggregate tend to choose poorly. Not for lack of ability, but more for a lack of paying attention. Marketing has a long tradition of duping its audience. Effective marketers skirt the credo, buyer beware, with ever better tools that tug at our insecurities, our longings, our lesser selves. And we as a buying public let them get away with it. We don't pay close attention to the detail: what's in our Fruit Loops, the ugly process that puts clothes on our backs, or the way financial markets are manipulated.

But ultimately we do get to decide what we buy and from whom we buy. The reasons we buy are born within what we believe—hence our collective opportunity to reshape the face of the planet.

Thankfully, there are already companies out there practicing social, environmental, ethical, and financial good. And, more and more, consumers are demanding that they do. Alarmingly, however, the bad outweighs the good and the good is coming at a snail's pace relative to the need. The reason: demand. The preponderance of consumers are still making bad choices, choices that cost us all dearly and spur on companies to continue to supply the ill-informed and ill-fated demand.

> "Those who plan for the future of their businesses, in every industry, have to take into account the increasing scarcity of energy and water and their rising cost, as well as the rising cost of waste and its disposal. Every company— from Walmart to the Cheese Board Collective, from BP to the makers of Fat Tire Ale, from Dow

Chemical to Patagonia—is already at work, in some way, even inadvertently, to dismantle a creaky, polluting, wasteful, and increasingly expensive industrial system, and is struggling to create new, less life-draining ways to make things; we are all trying to get a new roof up over the economy before the old, sagging one caves in."

YVON CHOUINARD AND VINCENT STANLEY
THE RESPONSIBLE COMPANY

But the old sagging one still has a stranglehold on the consuming public. And the quest to do the right thing is on the surface an expensive one, costly in old school metrics. These costs loom a stark and dramatic deterrent to change. Yet, quite a bit more costly are the coming metrics of resource scarcity and pollution.

But change is what we need. We are stuck, between a rock and a hard place, affording to do the right thing and affording to stay in business.

"To practice Right Livelihood, you have to find a way to earn your living without transgressing your ideals of love and compassion. The way you support yourself can be an expression of your deepest self, or it can be a source of suffering for you and others."

THICH NHAT HANH
THE HEART OF THE BUDDHA'S TEACHING

Through my years at Patagonia—and in my ten years of private consulting with over forty leading companies across a broad range of categories including apparel, outdoor, health and wellness, etcetera—I have developed a means by which to architect a loyal following called, in total, the Brand Ecosystem. This model substantiates and gives each and every company the unique understanding of what should and shouldn't be part of their landscape in order to engender a loyal constituency just their own. The Brand Ecosystem model is integral prior to branding, e-commerce development, social media strategies, marketing planning, everything. When done well, with an attention to detail and an objective eye, creative and marketing is no longer guesswork or dependent on inspired intuition, but lead by empirical data. The result is a roadmap that can be implemented to create loyal, long-term, sustainable customers. And the process is repeatable. The Brand Ecosystem model, as described in this book, encompasses all that a company needs to understand and express its purpose, engender rabidly loyal customers, and ultimately it's what I believe can potentially save the planet from the environmental crisis.

The more I consulted with clients, the more I put pen to paper crafting a book to explain the model, the more I began to realize there was a much more universal application than even a revolution in marketing technique. The ideas have proven to markedly improve businesses; however, the model's potential is in its application to larger systems.

The Brand Ecosystem model is what I was lucky enough to shepherd into existence during my tenure at Patagonia, and have since refined since its inception as an agent of change. Institutional change. Global change. It uses the science of advocacy to "do good" in the world, effecting positive change in a whole host of circumstances. For the purposes of this book, and because I personally am steeped in a history working with businesses practicing sustainability, it's aimed at leveraging the science of advocacy to wiggle us collectively out from between that rock and that hard place.

I love my work because it's transformative—helping good companies do better by architecting a state of sustainability through loyalty: sustainable environmentally, financially, and in relation to their customers, shareholders, vendors, and the biosphere as a whole. The larger mission emanating from my work on loyalty is a call to action for creating a better, more interconnected world; the creation of that world resides with establishing a new relationship between providers and users.

Venture capitalist and tech visionary Tim Draper, in a 2013 interview on NPR, observed that: "We need renovation in healthcare, government, and venture capital. That essentially these institutions are no longer viable and need [to be] rethought and redone." Draper neglected to mention education, Wall Street, and, more importantly, he neglects the elephant in the room, the fact that our economies will surely collapse if we curtail growth and our environment will assuredly cease to sustain us if we don't.

Reinventing and redesigning the fundamental relationships between providers of stuff and ourselves, the consumers of stuff, is our task; i.e., designing the Responsible Economy.

I don't remember a lot of detail from the day. I do remember the way I saw the world prior to Patagonia's

Cotton Tour and the way I saw the world after. My kids were one and three when I started working at Patagonia. My wife was passionate about raising them in as toxin-free of an environment as possible. That meant organic clothes and food, natural cleaners, soaps, shampoos, and, well, everything really. No easy task. It made perfect sense to us, though. Then I went on the Cotton Tour. And what had been a logical argument to us became an imperative for living that took on a meaning I never knew it could have.

The Cotton Tour was an opportunity made available to all employees. Patagonia provided it as part of the education about the environmental crisis that was paramount for all Patagonia employees to understand. It was also the basis for why Patagonia made the change to producing cotton products with only organic cotton and how the industry shifted in the nineties. Skeptics called it part of the Patagonia propaganda, but seeing it firsthand changed my life.

We boarded a twelve-passenger bus at sunrise at Patagonia's headquarters in Ventura, California and headed to California's Central Valley. The drive took us to a conventional cotton processing facility featuring a cotton gin, then to a conventional, industrial cotton farm, and finally to an organic cotton farm. We arrived back on campus at sundown the same day.

At that time, ten percent of all agricultural chemicals in the United States were used to produce cotton grown on just one percent of all major agricultural land. Conventional cotton crops in California alone were dusted every year with 6.9 million pounds of chemicals. Seeing a large-scale conventional cotton operation put those statistics into context very quickly. As we drove *through the valley, the plots of land extended over the horizon. It was stark; nothing was alive. That was what was most stark. Troughs ran around the perimeters of the "land," with trickles of water accumulating in them, but there were no weeds, grasses, shrubs, shade trees, birds, animals, or insects. Nothing but dirt-tinted gray. Much of the land is actually layered with clay tile that acts as a filter and allows excess water to drain into the hard dirt below, then into the ground water. The tile provides a base upon which layers of manufactured "soil" is distributed. The soil is trucked in from a soil creation facility that uses human waste as a starter material to create the muck in which the cotton plants are eventually grown. The cotton is harvested chemically, which promotes growth in a predator-free environment then kills the plant when it's ready for harvesting. The field is swept clean and the process begins again. Nothing grows on the land other than the cotton, and that for a brief period. Efficient I suppose, but the process is shockingly harsh, and because there is no real soil or plant diversity, the dust created in this area of the Central Valley has created horrendous air quality downwind in cities like Bakersfield. Bakersfield wins the award annually for the nation's worst air quality. I have family living in Bakersfield, and whenever I visit I'm reminded of the Cotton Tour because of the smell. Our sense of smell is linked to memory more so than any other sense, and to this day when I drive into the area the consistency of the smell triggers memories of the toxic day I spent touring the Central Valley cotton industry.*

The last few stops of the day took us to a couple of small organic farms. It was like discovering Oz. Life affirmed. Insects and weeds were beautiful. Color had returned to the world. I wasn't too intimidated to touch anything. And it smelled good.

The drive back to Ventura was long. I couldn't wait to get off the bus, get home, and take a shower. I wanted the smell of the Central Valley off of me. This was the day my life shifted. The environmental crisis was no longer an intellectual position that I held out of liberal politics, theory, and rhetoric. It became palpable for the first time in my life. Through the bus tour I literally experienced the destructiveness personally. I now embodied "cause no unnecessary harm." Patagonia was no longer a clothing brand to me. It was an entity that represented a transcendent purpose.

In 1972, Yvon Chouinard published his seminal catalog on "clean climbing." Little did anyone know that the approach of using business to positively effect the things he cared about would set Yvon Chouinard and his fledgling company, Patagonia, on course to becoming the tribal leader of the environmental movement in the outdoor industry and climbing community. And a key figure in the movement the world over. It all started with a disdain for defacing the mountains he climbed. In particular, the piton, a small piece of climbing equipment made of soft iron that was hammered into granite walls for climbers to affix their protective carabiners and ropes to, offended Chouinard. He not only considered the practice wrong for himself, as it damaged and scarred the rock walls, he challenged the global community to change their ways and did so in the opening pages of his very first product catalog, by proclaiming a new way to climb.

"There is a word for it, and the word is clean. Climbing with only nuts and runners for protection is clean climbing. Clean because the rock is left unaltered by the passing climber. Clean because nothing is hammered into the rock and then hammered back out, leaving the rock scarred and the next climber's experience less natural. Clean because the climber's protection leaves little track of his ascension. Clean is climbing the rock without changing it; a step closer to organic climbing for the natural man."

DOUG ROBINSON
"THE WHOLE NATURAL ART OF PROTECTION,"
1972 CHOUINARD EQUIPMENT CATALOG

Rather than continuing to produce the product that made up nearly 70% of his business' sales at the time he and his partner, Tom Frost, decided to phase out the piton from production and introduce an entirely new alternative, one that did no damage to the walls. Aluminum chocks were Chouinard's first risky move based on the principle of considering environmental impact. This bold stroke exceeded expectations as the climbing world acquiesced to the call. Within months, pitons were old news and chocks were being sold faster than they could be produced.

The catalog is known today as a "clean climbing manifesto," but in retrospect it was the beginning of a principled approach to doing business that has served the Chouinards and Patagonia for forty-plus years. Patagonia was the first in the United States to print its catalogs on recycled paper, the first to make fleece jackets using recycled plastic bottles, the first to offer on-campus day care, and the first company to use 100% organic cotton. In 2001, Chouinard cofounded 1% for the Planet, an alliance of companies, now numbering in the hundreds, committed to paying an "earth tax" of at least one percent of annual sales to environmental groups, as Patagonia has done since 1986. The list goes on and on, each decision harkening back to the original, and each steeped in principle.

The year 2013 marked Patagonia's 40th anniversary and they were at it again. That fall's catalog included another manifesto. This one eerily reminiscent of the first, entitled "The Elephant in the Room" and penned by Rick Ridgeway, Patagonia's VP of environmental affairs. It called for global change, a move away from our habits and our old ways of thinking and living. The article was in response to a forum on corporate sustainability where executives representing some of the world's largest global corporations such as Coca-Cola, Hewlett-Packard, and Walmart, presented what their respective companies were doing to behave more responsibly and sustainably. In Ridgeway's estimation, all of the presentations were in one form or another related to innovation, and in most cases had been in the works for years; he thought the efforts "were laudable." Yet the elephant in the room, the one thing no one truly wanted to speak to, was the conundrum "that our businesses continue to depend on annual, compounded growth, and growth was overriding the incremental benefits from the new technologies." Essentially, technology is not solving the problem, nor will it in the foreseeable future. Therefore, just as Chouinard called for change in 1973, Ridgeway, and

Patagonia, are calling for change again. They are asking the global community of businesses and consumers to rally around an idea they've coined the Responsible Economy, in the hope that the effects of the past can be curbed and humanity can secure the future of the biosphere.

Patagonia is not alone wrestling with the fact that the global economy's wellbeing is predicated on growth, and yet it is the result of that growth, our population's growth, and our irrespective stewardship of the wellbeing of the biosphere that we find virtually all forms of life threatened. In fact, in an anthology edited by Allan Hunt Badiner in 2002 entitled *Mindfulness in the Marketplace,* Badiner suggests "a reorientation of consumers from passive purchasers to aware, responsible citizens who see the dynamic connection between their purchases and their values."

And it is Sir Richard Branson and Jochen Zeitz' B Team, launched in 2013, that challenges business leaders to work together to deliver a new way of doing business that prioritizes people and planet alongside profit, "a Plan B for businesses the world over."

There are also tangible efforts that have been in the works for years, working at the ground level of product production. The 2002 book, *Cradle to Cradle: Remaking the Way We Make Things,* by German chemist Michael Braungart and US architect William McDonough, is a manifesto in its own right that details the theory of zero-impact product production, further invigorated by Ellen MacArthur's Foundation promoting the Circular Economy.

Unfortunately, the finger waving, pontificating, theorizing, and philosophizing only gets us to a broad awareness at best. Regardless of the good intention of these and the many others working for the common good, they are mostly speaking to an audience that already understands the issue. The predominance of our global population is in no way capable, even if they were clearly aware of the problem, to enact the type of conservationist behavior on a daily basis that will effect a positive enough change on the order of magnitude required to stop, repair, and revitalize the ruin.

So, how do we reach the larger population? Where do we go from here? Ridgeway even asks, "Is there a solution?" I believe there is, and it resides in the discipline and practice of design, loyalty architecture, and a new model that facilitates the connection between purchases and values. The Brand Ecosystem model sits at the apex of Einstein's prescient comment summarizing our circumstance: "The perfection of means and confusion of aims seem to be our main problem." In simpler terms, it's a user experience problem.

This book is an answer to the problem. The human race is just now facing having to relearn how to live within the means provided by the planet. Science and technology require ethics so that technology can properly serve humanity and the planet; however, most of our problems need to be solved by understanding one another's beliefs and values, and the cognitive processes they influence. The Brand Ecosystem model takes all of these things into account.

In the pages that follow, you will learn what is at the root of loyalty and the phenomenon of following. You will learn how forming a near unbreakable bond to a brand, organization, political party, or cause happens, and how that process can be leveraged to fix our user experience problem. It will absolutely help businesses understand and engender customer loyalty as a means to grow and profit. It also illustrates a process for understanding the connection between that loyalty and sustainability. And it just may be our greatest opportunity to create a new Responsible, Circular Economy, and an Empathic Civilization.

**"All our knowledge begins
with the senses, proceeds
then to the understanding,
and ends with reason."**

IMMANUEL KANT

CHAPTER TWO

Choosing to See

I have an uncontrollable knack for dissecting systems. It's the coach in me. My previous consulting partner said my single most valuable asset is my ability to turn things upside down and inside out. I long to create a fruitful path to improving on the status quo, and sometimes upsetting the status quo can upset those on the receiving end of the analysis. That is the risk inherent in my work. I'm a "loyalty architect." When I engage with a company and its customers to improve their relationship, I see things the way a chef, doctor, or an architect sees their world. Chefs learn to discern subtle ingredients, doctors learn to understand nuances in their patient's responses to stimulus, architects learn to see space in the context of structure and good user experience. I see nuances: the nuances of communication, of marketing, and of branding brought into focus from years of honing my senses. I see the cognitive processes underlying the customer's choices in relationship to the particular brand I'm working. I see where there is resonance. I see disconnects. I see the biases at work in the company—in the individuals and teams responsible for managing the very marketing programs they are objectively trying to optimize for the good of the organization.

The word "resonance" is key. I'm drawn to the definition used as applied to mechanics: *The condition in which an object or system is subjected to an oscillating force having a frequency close to its own natural frequency.* I am moved by the idea that there is a natural frequency that exists objectively. It speaks to my experience and the observations I make in my work. It's why Patagonia customers buy Patagonia and not The North Face, or Cloudveil, or Columbia, or Mountain Hardware. Patagonia is an oscillating force with a frequency close to their customer's "natural frequency."

Noise that covers up the natural connection between frequencies, unfortunately, is what I mostly encounter when I look at a typical company's marketing and branding. The noise is all of the machinations the business managers put forth in hopes of manipulating a customer to do what they want them to do, what the creative marketing teams do to attempt to manipulate the emotions and actions of their customers: calls to action information overload, endless features and benefits, up sells, cross sells, promotions, recommendations, testimonials, reviews, superfluous "content," and likely the most pervasive source of noise—promotional advertising.

My ongoing frustration is with the superficiality of brands. They often communicate to consumers in overly simplistic terms, dumbing down the truth to persuade rather than inform. I find it disrespectful. The fact is that because this gnaws at me, I suppose it's part of the reason I've been motivated to discover a model for marketing that is mutually respectful and that aligns customer frequency with company frequency. It's also why this book's title references Sir Walter Scott's penchant for a true compass. Brands invariably stray from their true North for all sorts of desperate reasons— the noise, the rusty nail, steering them off course.

An example of the noise, the superficiality, is the output of the analytics providers. Adobe, IBM, and the rest of the marketing analytics world drone on and on in their marketing campaigns about would-be clients not knowing what their marketing is doing. Adobe famously asks, "Do you know what your marketing is doing?"

The irony is not lost on me: These providers have no idea what their own marketing is doing, yet they ask the question of other companies with a tone of accession.

They might have lots of data, and that data might provide statistical evidence that one marketing vehicle is working better than another, that one message could outperform another, or that a particular layout on a Web site converts higher than another. But they can't tell you what resonates at a deep level with a customer and causes that customer to commit to a long-term sustainable relationship with any brand, let alone their own brand in particular.

I'm not arguing that A/B testing isn't a great tool, or usability testing in general isn't handy, or that detailed analysis of funnel conversion rates isn't insightful, or that the myriad of other marketing and CRM (Customer Relationship Management) packages aren't smart business. I'm arguing that all of these efforts overlook what really matters. They are superficial. They don't create loyalty. They don't create understanding of customers' natural frequencies.

In the late nineties and early part of the twenty-first century, personalized marketing was all the rage—provide a customized message and experience for each of your customers (a personal email, a product selection, and an offer unique to a given customer) based specifically on predetermined needs. It's still the general thinking today. Netflix recommends movies based on user habits, Amazon is obviously doing the same, and every other small- and medium-sized business is chasing a similar dream: personalized, one-to-one marketing.

Sadly, the success of monolithic brands like Walmart and Amazon have somehow convinced marketers that those models are the gold standard, that efficiency of pricing models, advertising, and promotions are the clubs that bludgeon customers into submission. It's disheartening. Not because these methods win, but because the unsuspecting public allows them to win. We gravitate like lemmings to the short-term windfall but regret the eventual outcome every time. Short-term gratification is what these marketers prey on, and even for them it's not sustainable. Eventually, we'll exhaust ourselves as consumers of mere price and convenience and demand something more. Something better. Something sustainable. And so, to take the steps necessary to get there, the rest of us marketers need a new model to compete against the monoliths. And we consumers need something more than the qualities of price and convenience.

I created the Brand Ecosystem, which we'll explore in the rest of this book, to help my clients understand that there is a more effective way. This new model combats the victimization of the average consumer by showing companies how to reach audiences in much more meaningful ways, and giving consumers a means to glean the truth about their purchase choices that actually matter to them.

Customers are individuals, and when given an opportunity to consider who they are buying from, what the people they buy from believe, and their own active responsibility in that equation, they will choose belief over all other attributes, which in turn is a greater measurement of value than price.

> "We don't see things as they are, we see them as we are."
>
> ANAÏS NIN

We see the world the way we've been shaped to see it, interpret it, and understand it. This is true of statistics and quantitative study, but especially true of qualitative study. We are always at risk of seeing the results we wish to see and are conditioned to see, subconsciously ignoring evidence to the contrary. Daniel Kahneman and Amos Tversky, the famous psychologists, developed the series of experiments to test cognitive bias that proved exactly that.

Seeing accurately, without a bias, requires a framework for observation. Once we firmly establish a framework to assess data, feedback, and empirical evidence, we increase our accuracy, our ability to judge, and our ability to conceive of solutions to problems. This is the value of the Brand Ecosystem. It is a framework to understand your customer and how they come to understand you. It's also a framework for design, specifically the design of user experiences.

> "User experience encompasses all aspects of the end-user's interaction with the company, its services, and its products. The first requirement for an exemplary user experience is to meet the exact needs of the customer,

without fuss or bother. Next comes simplicity and elegance that produce products that are a joy to own, a joy to use. True user experience goes far beyond giving customers what they say they want, or providing checklist features. In order to achieve high-quality user experience in a company's offerings there must be a seamless merging of the services of multiple disciplines, including engineering, marketing, graphical and industrial design, and interface design."

JAKOB NIELSEN AND DON NORMAN[i]

We humans are interpretive beings. We see things based on our histories, practices, professions, beliefs, biases, and emotional states in any given moment. We design from our own personal perspectives and agendas. Subjectivity is a paramount influence in the design process. This serves us well when we hone the senses.

The idea that our perception is influenced as much by what we know as it is by what we think we know is well-known social science. This notion affects the accuracy of what we know because what we know is influenced by what we expect to find.

"Up to now it has been assumed that all our cognition must conform to the objects; but [...] let us once try whether we do not get further [...] by assuming that the objects must conform to our cognition."

IMMANUEL KANT
CRITIQUE OF PURE REASON

---

i   Jakob Nielsen and Don Norman, "The Definition of User Experience," Nielsen Norman Group, www.nngroup.com/articles/definition-user-experience/

In other words, be cautious about focusing on what you want customers (users) to do. We see customers from the point of view of marketers. We are hoping customers do what we want them to do and behave the way we want them to behave. If we were to simply step away from our own desires as marketers and attempt to know our customers more objectively, we would discover characteristics, needs, beliefs, and behaviors that are completely different from what we thought we knew, and something completely different than what we had hoped.

Our ability to discern the truth about the data we process is affected by what cognitive psychologists call a Perceptual Set.[ii]

> "Perceptual Set is a tendency to perceive or notice some aspects of the available sensory data and ignore others. Perceptual Set works in two ways:
>
> 1. The perceiver has certain expectations and focuses attention on particular aspects of the sensory data [...]
>
> 2. The perceiver knows how to classify, understand and name selected data and what inferences to draw from it [...]."
>
> SAUL MCLEOD
> THE PERCEPTUAL SET

---

ii   "The Perceptual Set," Information Architects, ia.net/know-how/learning-to-see

The way expectation can influence our cognitive set can be illustrated quite easily:

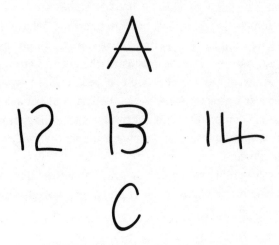

Depending on how you read the diagram, you will read the characters in the middle as "13" or "B."

"The physical stimulus '13' is the same in each case but is perceived differently because of the influence of the context in which it appears. We EXPECT to see a letter in the context of other letters of the alphabet, whereas we EXPECT to see numbers in the context of other numbers."

IBID.

The influence of past experience on perception can be demonstrated in the following puzzling experience:

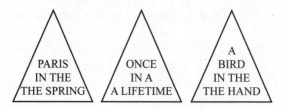

Because past experience of hearing or reading these common phrases can influence your perception, you ignore the errors that seem obvious once they are revealed. In this case:

"...we don't see that we don't see."

HUMBERTO R. MATURANA AND FRANCISCO VARELA
THE TREE OF KNOWLEDGE

Our Perceptual Set can change short-term, for instance when we are hungry our sensitivity to the smell of food is strengthened. The way experience affects long-term perceptual sets can be studied by analyzing the different perceptive sets of professionals that are strongly influenced by what they know.

- Cooks and sommeliers are able to more clearly discern what they taste because, through constant exposure, they have improved senses, and also the vocabulary to express and discuss their impressions.

- When doctors look at X-rays, they see more because they know anatomy and what to look for in the mix of light and shadow. Over the years they have learned to more clearly discern slight differences in shape and shade that to us are indiscernible.

- When an architect enters a building, they see through the walls, and they understand the building as a four-dimensional space-time continuum.

- When fashion designers look at your outfit, they don't simply see stylish clothes, they see cut, seam, and material. They imagine how your clothes feel.

Marketers, sales people, and business managers live in highly contextualized environments as well. They are influenced by lots of varying stimuli and pressures:

- Making next quarter's sales numbers

- Proving the value of hard won strategic initiatives

- Justifying budgets to bosses, CFOs, Private Equity partners, etcetera

- Justifying marketing expenditures with performance metrics

- Achieving performance-based bonuses and promotions

A list of this sort can go on and on. Ultimately, these types of pressures create biases that influence our abilities to assess the truth. In the midst of these circumstances, we are truly choosing what we see. And beyond this surface interpretation, we go further and manipulate this information, sometimes customizing it, to fit our needs. This, the rusty nail that wrecks the argosy.

This cognitive trickery is pervasive in human behavior and, thus, in business behavior, economic behavior, and in many structures, systems, and services. Knowing these mental gymnastics exist allows us to look deeper into potential solutions. Take, for example, Nava Ashraf's interesting look at behavioral economics through this lens:

> "Why doesn't a woman who continues to have unwanted pregnancies avail herself of the free contraception at a nearby clinic? What keeps people from using free chlorine tablets to purify their drinking water? Behavioral economics has shown us that we don't always act in our own best interests. This is as true of health decisions as it is of economic ones. An array of biases, limits on cognition, and motivations lead people all over the world to make suboptimal health choices. The good news is that human nature can also be a source of solutions. Through her studies in Zambia exploring the reasons for unwanted pregnancies and the incentives that would motivate hairdressers to sell condoms to their clients, the author has found that designing effective health programs requires more than providing accessible, affordable care; it requires understanding what makes both end users and providers tick. By understanding the cognitive processes underlying our choices and applying the tools of behavioral economics—such as commitment devices, material incentives, defaults, and tools

that tap our desire to help others—it's possible to design simple, inexpensive programs that encourage good health decisions and long-term behavior change."

NAVA ASHRAF
"RX: HUMAN NATURE: HOW BEHAVIORAL ECONOMICS IS PROMOTING BETTER HEALTH AROUND THE WORLD"
HARVARD BUSINESS SCHOOL

While it may seem incongruous to talk about healthcare decisions in the context of the changing face of marketing and customer behavior, both are part of a larger endeavor to design more sustainable systems based on the greater good. Remember Nava Ashraf's words aligning human behavior, that creating resonance "...requires understanding what makes both end users and providers tick. By understanding the cognitive processes underlying our choices...it's possible to design, simple, inexpensive programs that encourage good health and decisions and long-term behavior change." And, in our circumstance, for our purposes, understanding what makes both end users and providers tick is where the sweet spot of loyalty resides.

By understanding the journey your best customers take to become your best customer you can remove the guesswork from your creative. You can understand exactly the messages that resonate the most, the experiences your advocates have had that matter most, the product attributes they value most, and the most important reason they support your brand. If you truly know this in advance of developing your communications campaign and designing your customer's user experience and customer service experience, you can effectively tell the story that will move your customers to understanding rather than just trying to get them to do what you want. New customers will become repeat customers and those repeat customers will become advocates much more seamlessly if their journey is understood and mapped logically and rationally. Think of this as the "physical architecture of loyalty," in terms of the model, it can also be described as the Progression of Resonance.

The discipline of design touches virtually every aspect of our lives, the subtleties of visionary design create touchstones for the provider and the user to connect.

These touch points are more than just the pragmatic user needs that create or disable satisfaction between a consumer and a business. One can clearly see them addressing intangible emotional triggers in settings where the user is less a defining factor of success. The leap here is not just in crafting well-wrought user experience design for businesses in order to nurture satisfaction and a relationship with core consumers, but also for providers of any sort to craft optimum human interactive experience: designs of cities managing congestion, designers of student curricula in education, architects of government services, political platforms, and even economic policy.

"We have to recognize that there cannot be relationships unless there is commitment, unless there is loyalty, unless there is love, patience, persistence."

CORNEL WEST

CHAPTER THREE

WHY MATTERS:
The Basis for Inspired Relationships

Before we can explore the foundation for architecting loyalty—the how to do it and the what to do—we need to explore what defines'long-term, sustainable loyalty. The distinguishing characteristic is the relationship between an audience of users and a provider of some perceived value. If this relationship exists, the force that's acting on that relationship is steeped in aligned beliefs and is based on mutual trust and inspiration. We have to understand our own beliefs and purpose before we can connect with others about them. We need to know why we do what we do before we can explain how we do it or what we do. This is true for any type of organization whether it's a business, a political party, a charity, or even institutional systems such as healthcare, education, or economic policy.

In his book *Start With Why*, Simon Sinek argues that "inspired organizations and people all think, act, and communicate from the inside out." They inspire, enact followers, become leaders, and succeed because they connect to their constituents on a more primal, emotional level of the limbic brain where feelings, trust, and loyalty reside and drive our behavior. Rather than communicate rationally about what we do, when we communicate on the level of emotion about why we do it, we connect with others with greater impact. In Simon's words, "...if you don't know why you do what you do, then how will you ever get someone to buy into it, and be loyal, or want to be a part of what it is that you do?" Sinek continues with shining examples of Martin Luther King Jr. and Steve Jobs, demonstrating the cognitive processes behind their leadership.

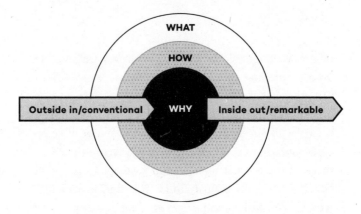

The diagram depicts Sinek's Golden Circle and describes an enlightened way to look at problems and business models globally and locally. It's simple, really. We normally work from the what to the how to the why, letting outside forces decide and define what matters. Sinek shows that if we start with the why, with our purpose for doing something, the how and the what follow from a more centered, inspired place.

Simon Sinek's Golden Circle helps us understand how leaders succeed in gaining a following. Instead of just talking about this model theoretically, instead of lamenting about whether we may or may not have the oratory chops of Martin Luther King Jr. or the vision of Steve Jobs, we can actually apply a deliberate, easy to implement, process that allows all of us to lead a cause, create loyalty in a business, or create the change we want to see in the world.

Dan Pallotta is the president of Advertising for Humanity. They help foundations and philanthropists transform the growth potential of their favorite grantees. He's best known for creating the multiday charitable event industry, and a new generation of citizen philanthropists with the AIDS Rides and Breast Cancer 3-Day events, which raised $582 million over a nine-year stint. Unfortunately, at the end of his tenure creating these milestone fundraising events, his organization went bankrupt. He tells the story in a popular TED Talk, "The Way We Think About Charity is Dead Wrong."

When he was in the midst of revolutionizing the way charities could raise money and succeeding wildly at doing so, he was also making a profit for himself and his then-company, Pallotta TeamWorks. What he didn't realize at the time was the intense moral position the American public held against the idea that someone could profit from managing charitable donations.

He notes, "We have a visceral reaction to the idea that anyone would make very much money helping other people." His TED Talk goes on to present the conundrum he faced while losing his business: "Interesting that we don't have a visceral reaction to the notion that people would make a lot of money not helping other people"; meaning that we as a public don't concern ourselves with Xbox making a fortune from producing violent video game content, but we shudder at the thought of recruiting talent into the nonprofit world with competitive salaries to succeed at managing and funding cause-related nonprofits. He goes on to note, "You want to make fifty million dollars making violent video games [for] kids, go for it, we'll put you on the cover of *Wired* magazine, but you want to make half a million dollars trying to cure kids of Malaria and you're considered a parasite yourself."

In the end, Dan Pallotta's early foray into the world of nonprofit failed, for one simple reason: He didn't understand the qualities of the belief system of his constituents, the American public. He understands them today, but he paid a hefty price to figure it out. Dan Pallotta's business is a classic case of providing a great service (he raised well beyond his promised performance for the charities he was contracted) and running a well organized business (by all accounts he ran an efficient company with high-quality people loyal to the business), but ultimately failing because he did not operate at the intersection of a shared belief system. Dan Pallotta is a remarkably successful guy. He graduated from Harvard, he's a successful entrepreneur, author, a humanitarian activist, and today he's living testament that people don't buy what you do, they buy why you do it. He now resides almost exclusively in purpose.

> "'The nonprofit sector is critical to our dream of changing the world. Yet there is no greater injustice than the double standard that exists between the for-profit and nonprofit sectors. One gets to feast on marketing, risk-taking, capital and financial incentive, the other is sentenced to begging,' Dan Pallotta says in discussing his latest book, *Charity Case*. This economic starvation of our nonprofits is why he believes we are not moving the needle on great

social problems. 'My goal...is to fundamentally transform the way the public thinks about charity within ten years.'"

TED[iii]

"The next time you're looking at a charity, don't ask about the rate of their overhead. Ask about the scale of their dreams."

DAN PALLOTTA[iv]

Dan Pallotta now works from a place of purpose. He has defined his beliefs, namely that the way we think about charity holds us back and we need to change it. That is very different from simply going about doing something new, doing the how and the what, without first embracing the why. In Pallotta's case, to begin with the why will help him inspire the change he was unable to when he didn't offer people a purpose or point of connection.

This is the decisive moment: Clearly establishing a foothold understanding where your organization's values intersect with your audience, then digging into the detail as a means to create process and an operating principle to move forward. This is the new means to create lasting value in the relationship between an organization of any kind and the people it serves; applied to politics, economic strategies, causes, businesses, etcetera. It's a universal truth.

For ages, branding and marketing experts have based their success on identifying demographic

iii   "The Way We Think About Charity is Dead Wrong," TED, March 2013. www.ted .com/speakers/dan_pallotta

iv   Ibid.

segments and presenting these segments with a well-wrought value proposition. This served Madison Avenue well, but the game has changed. This model is too superficial and lacks meaning today. The value proposition today serves really only as a first impression because customers have the world at their fingertips. They have other consumers reviewing and commenting on service, quality, durability, etcetera. They can comparison shop across distribution channels for price and delivery. And, most importantly, consumers today weigh the "value proposition" as much based on who's making the product as the value the product provides alone. This is the real change that Rick Levine alluded to back at the turn of the century in his seminal marketing book, *The Cluetrain Manifesto*. Levine stated very clearly that the corporate veil was systematically being removed and the consumer would be back in control of the marketplace. That the consumer would know who was growing their tomatoes, which vendor could be trusted, and who was delivering their goods at a fair price. Well, his prophetic words were spot on. Unfortunately, most marketers didn't listen.

The vast number of brands and products marketed today are still presented with that veiled attempt to claim to be the best, outperforming the competition with features and benefits. What somehow everyone missed is that the path to long-term, sustainable loyalty is based on an unspoken agreement: *You believe what I believe and I believe what you believe. Now we can do business from a place of trust and inspiration.*

It's the reason customers of The North Face don't wear Patagonia and customers of Patagonia don't wear The North Face. Not because of features and benefits, style or color, price or service, but because if you believe in conquering nature, you're likely a fan of The North Face. If you believe in the value of being in nature, you're likely a fan of Patagonia.

The crux of the matter is identifying the intersection of what the organization believes and what the consumer believes. How the brand delivers its product or service relative to that belief system and how the customer's need is satisfied more uniquely because of that belief. This is what enables a successful, long-term business relationship.

For the service provider, defining, communicating, and supporting an aligned relationship between themselves as the provider and the consumer and recognizing exactly what a provider is relative to the consumer needs to be the focus. We know the consumer is the person consuming the product or service. We often think of the provider simply in terms of business, in terms of a for-profit entity that exchanges goods and services for some monetary return. This limits our worldview and limits the application of this thinking. A service provider is any entity that delivers value, or perceived value, to a user. The traditional example includes businesses as straightforward as a restaurant. McDonald's provides a perceived value in exchange for a relatively small amount of money for a meal. A five-star restaurant such as Noma's in Denmark provides an entirely unique experience with an on-campus garden and dishes prepared by award winning chefs based on the season's bounty. Both are restaurants. Both provide a value in exchange for a monetary return. Beyond this strict definition of a business, however, we need to explore entities that provide value but don't strictly provide a monetary return to the organization. These would include nonprofits, charities, political parties, governments, sports teams, broadcast networks, and lots and lots of online services.

Now that we have looked at why loyalty, inspiration, mutual trust, shared values, and purpose are important to businesses and organizations, we can take a look at how we architect our business to reflect this sense of shared purpose.

"Character is like a tree and
reputation like a shadow;
the shadow is what we think of
it; the tree is the real thing."

ABRAHAM LINCOLN

CHAPTER FOUR

HOW MATTERS:

The Brand Ecosystem

So here we stand at the precipice of something greater, the means to reveal the character in the relationship between customers and companies. What follows is an overview of the model that explains what great companies do to engender long-term sustainable relationships with very distinct customer segments, and an accounting of what creates resonance at a deep level with a single customer, and therefore an entire segment of customers.

The first step is knowing how to strike a common understanding between providers and users. As obvious as that might seem, there is no underestimating how important it is to establish that common ground. But it's not about the obvious benefit we assume the user gets, and it's not about marketers frivolously attempting to convince us they are better than their competitors. It's about digging much deeper than we ever have before. To uncover something that matters.

The type of design environment explored in the coming pages is specific to the business/consumer design effort because there is less of a quantitative measure of success in nonbusiness settings. In business we have the all-powerful transaction putting control ultimately in the hands of the consumer. Without this metric—as in, say, a public education or government service agency setting—the user is essentially without a voice and without a vote. Even in a political arena voters are often marginalized, or worse, disenfranchised. This is when it becomes imperative for the designers, the architects, to employ the qualitative application of empathy, to design for user needs. By integrating the motivations and emotional states of the user, we can create an optimal end user experience regardless of the tangible transactional metric. Because it's the right thing to do.

What many great leaders do naturally, or what many great companies do naturally, the rest of us can learn to do deliberately. It's not mystical. In fact, it's practical, even scientific. The question to be answered is: How can some companies create such strong affection for their brands that their customers feel compelled to rave about them?

All companies would love to have the loyalty some of the iconic brands exhibit. Apple, Patagonia, and Harley Davidson are just a few examples of brands with intensely loyal customers who stand by them through thick and thin, even in lean times.

Why do fans of Harley Davidson swear by the brand even though it has never laid claim to being the best motorcycle in the world? They've never claimed to be the best performing, best engineered, most durable— nor best anything, really—yet Harley Davidson engenders a rabid fan base that exudes a love for their brand that spans decades. Somehow they create value beyond simply product quality, features, and benefits.

If we can identify the brands with the greatest loyalty, can we copy these iconic brands? Can we look at their marketing plans, their organizational structure, their leadership, their service, product development, and branding, and glean some secret that each and every one of these companies harbor as if they were all members of some underground club that understands success better and differently than the rest of us? No.

If we can't copy them, can we at least use their approaches as models? Not really. Science teaches us that if you repeat circumstances and variables you'll see similar results. In business, it's near impossible to isolate all of the variables. Emulation is an inherently flawed approach. In fact, the most volatile variable in the equation is almost always the actual leadership of the organization. Just as in the scientific method, we recognize that the observer can actually change the results of the experiment. Regardless of who you are, or what your circumstance, you can't be Steve Jobs. You have to be you. You have to lead in your own way, deal with your own circumstances, and manage within your market uniquely.

The Brand Ecosystem model made up of the Customer Activation Cycle and Story Universe uncover what matters most: experiences, communications, beliefs, information, and values. The model unearths and exposes those things. It reveals resonance. The Customer Activation Cycle puts definition to that resonance and distinguishes the key components that forge a long-lasting relationship. These key customer experiences rise above the traditional marketing noise; sifting out what matters and separating it from the noise is a process of discovery and discipline. But bringing the character of the organization to the forefront is not enough. In order to design a system that compels an individual to become a Brand Advocate, to engage completely, it's imperative to come to understand deeply what makes both end users and providers tick. It is then and only then that we can design a user experience from start to finish that best facilitates that relationship and exposes a company's character in meaningful ways to the end user.

Nature provides the proof point.

In order to organize complex systems, whether they are animal, plant, or mineral, there is always an organizing principle at play that trumps circumstance. Variable environments, competitive influences, and a multitude of threats exist, yet living beings find a way to not only survive, but also to thrive. They do so because they follow the principles that determine success or failure. Biologists know that within a certain range of circumstances (an ecosystem), a given organizing principle driving a system will net a predictable result, statistically speaking, which means close to 100%. We can apply this to learning how success and rabid loyalty happens. The trick is that in any given situation there is an appropriate principle upon which the organization can stake its claim.

> "A designer knows he has achieved perfection not when there is nothing left to add, but when there is nothing left to take away."
>
> **ANTOINE DE SAINT-EXUPERY**

Patagonia became the leader in its category not because of environmentalism, but because of a design philosophy that maintained seventeen distinct design principles, the key principle being about simplicity. The net result of that one principle includes non-obsolescence, a simplified mass production process, lower cost of goods, greater durability, ease of use, and ultimately higher customer satisfaction. Yvon Chouinard succeeded not because he was a shrewd businessman or even a champion of the environment, but because he was steeped in principle. "Build the best product, cause no unnecessary harm..." This is not a slogan, nor a position, or an attempt to be the best. It's a driving principle that by definition results in product that is of value only when it does as little harm to the environment as possible in its production and in its intended use.

> "Who are businesses really responsible to? Their customers? Shareholders? Employees? We would argue that it's none of the above. Fundamentally, businesses are responsible to their resource base. Without a healthy environment there are no shareholders, no employees, no customers and no business."
>
> PATAGONIA AD SERIES

In my years of work with Patagonia, I discovered there is a thread that runs through their belief system that judges humanity pretty harshly. The best word to capture that thread is odium. It's a fitting word to describe how Patagonia judges our actions as a global society, actions that have brought about the environmental crisis. Our continuing disregard for our own habitat is confounding. To work at Patagonia meant understanding that this judgment is woven into everything.

Once your point of view shifts, once you understand things you were previously ignorant of, it becomes hard to tolerate the old way of thinking. Empathetic to those who haven't shifted their awareness, yes, but entirely tolerant of their behavior—not in the case of environmental protection, because environmental protection is a pragmatic point of view. We live in a fragile bubble.

Reverence for nature is inherent in the Patagonia ethos, an ethos born from a connection to nature through experience. It seems odd that people have to make an effort to understand what it means to bond or connect with nature. It wasn't that long ago we all lived directly off the land. Maybe this is at the heart of the local, organic, slow food movement. Maybe it's at the heart of the age-old question, "Why climb a mountain?," and its ubiquitous answer, "Because it's there." Sailors, surfers, climbers, and all manner of outdoor enthusiasts pine for "the great outdoors," but maybe not in the terms that are often depicted (in terms of conquering), but rather in terms of communion with something from which we are practically removed—our connection to nature—by our living conditions (insulated houses, paved streets, noiseproof cars, etcetera). The ethos that founded Patagonia was a reverence for nature's beauty, intelligence, and interconnectedness, its system architecture, a healthy fascination with the fact that all things are dependent on all other things. At the core of this is the recognition that everything is in interplay, which in my estimation is why athletes delve so deeply into their particular sport passions, to touch that interplay, to gain some better, more meaningful connection to the natural forces at work, whether they are rock, water, or air. It's what drew me to the idea of "natural frequency."

There is a subtle difference between knowing this interdependency, this interplay, this frequency, and not knowing it. Once known, the clarity is stark. Once experience enlightens an individual, explaining is no longer necessary. At Patagonia, the dividing line is a harsh, thick one. There is little tolerance of crossing it or residing on the wrong side of it. Accordingly, there is no real moral decision. There's just one right thing to do. It's an ethical code: Do the least harm.

The challenge with Patagonia as an example is that it's an iconic brand, but it didn't start out that way. It didn't come into existence with an interest in competing, or even in contrast with competitors, or to even be a business. It wasn't about any of those things. People tend to think of it like an Apple case study, something to be emulated, copied, modeled, and duplicated. The brand is the way it is, literally, because of an internal point of view that is steadfastly believed in and is all-consuming. It is impossible to emulate exactly because too many things went into making it that way and because it is born from a specific place, time, and set of ideas.

This is why reading endlessly about examples of success stories like Patagonia is inspirational, but impossible to repeat. Trying to repeat it misses the point—values aren't something you copy from someone else, they come from the inside out. Uncovering, understanding, and constructing organizing principles upon which your business can make decisions over the long haul is the place to focus. Defining the organizing principles for your organization from the supply chain all the way through to the the end-user experience becomes paramount.

It's this kind of principled decision making that creates success. Thomas Edison did not set out to invent a lightbulb, to create a light. He wasn't looking to found a company. He was motivated by a cause and driven by a principle. He believed in an egalitarian distribution of electricity, that society would be better served if electricity could be distributed inexpensively to the masses, and he needed to demonstrate it. The lightbulb was the proof point. The same principle-driven decision-making created Henry Ford's production line. He was seeking an affordable solution for mass transit, and mass production of the automobile was the solution. Steve Jobs' principle, "Put the power of information in the hands of the people," is another incarnation. The examples are endless. The point is that none of these amazing success stories can ever be repeated. As much as we want to study them and learn from them we can't repeat them. But for some reason our media and the managerial masses have this notion they can rub a bit of Steve Jobs off on themselves and create some groundbreaking business model. It just won't happen.

What *can* happen is a defining of the principle that consistently self-organizes solutions. This is where we will change the game: in principle. The work is to architect the organization such that the principles manifest in everything it does.

The Science of Building Advocacy

I've been an entrepreneur and marketer for a very long time. All the while holding a deep curiosity for why "loyalty" happens. With experience, I've come to be a believer in system thinking and the power of organizing principles. What follows is a scientific model that explains loyalty in architectural form. It organizes a brand's character so that it manifests in the detail of a user's interaction, which nets a uniquely powerful, one-of-a-kind experience that aligns with the cognitive processes of that individual user. It is this alignment that makes loyalty happen. And it's my passion today, architecting loyal user behavior in any brand, product, or service environment.

Having worked across a broad variety of brands, categories, and business models, one thing has become abundantly evident: There is not a clear industry definition of why loyalty happens, why a customer becomes loyal and stays committed to a brand relationship. There are endless articles about loyalty, the effects of service, product, pricing, etcetera. There are vast CRM technologies and applications from Adobe, IBM, Microsoft, Salesforce, and many others that collect, crunch, and report data. There are the old school direct marketers measuring recency, frequency, and monetary metrics, and the new school digital wunderkinds that spend countless hours and dollars optimizing for conversion, average order value, click-thru, and churn reduction. There are even proof points of loyalty, such as the infamous NPI (Net Promoter Index), first made public by *Harvard Business Review* recounting how Enterprise Rent-a-Car scaled its business faster than any competitor in the ever-crowded car rental category by closely monitoring customer satisfaction as a metric. But no one is testing for *why* loyalty happens. Without an empirical definition of the process of loyalty, all other definitions of performance are meaningless because they don't identify the difference maker between potential and capacity. What is the psychographic, physiological, monetary difference between potential and capacity? Why is it that some customers discover a brand and become loyal to that brand? None of the metrics, applications, or reporting laundry listed above can identify or measure the rate at which a potential customer migrates to a state of advocacy. The models described here do exactly this.

The Customer Activation Cycle and the Story Universe define loyalty in scientific terms, making why loyalty happens measurable, predictable, observable, and repeatable. It's a measurement of the holistic health of advocacy creation. This is the only true CRM methodology in existence today. It predicts loyalty. It is as complete a definition as there has ever been.

Testing for the Rate of Migration from the moment a customer is introduced to a brand to the moment that customer commits to a long-term relationship yields an understanding about loyal behavior that trumps all other measurements. In the other myriad disciplines, KPIs (Key Performance Metrics), metrics, and methods of data analysis, and other particular measurements of performance, the small pieces of the larger context are understood. The flaw in testing disparate particular pieces and parts rather than the whole occurrence, however, is that no single interaction, no single event, dictates success or failure.

The evolution of a loyal customer does not follow a linear path. This is critical when predicting loyalty of any kind, be it between a brand and its customer, a donor base and a nonprofit, a political candidate and their constituency, or even an educational system and its students. There is a progression to it, an accretive forming of loyalty over time. The experiences are haphazard, cross media, and relational in nature. Any single occurrence may or may not test well, but that doesn't indicate the likelihood of loyalty. Random events altogether must be accounted for, organized, and operationalized to truly understand how well loyalty is forming. This is what the Customer Activation Cycle and the Story Universe together do as a CRM methodology.

It's best to distinguish between a company's character and the things it makes to explain how these models work. IBM exemplifies the difference. Over their one hundred-plus year history, IBM has made a remarkably diverse array of product, including scales, clocks, meat slicers, cheese slicers, typewriters, and mainframe computers, to name just a few. Admittedly, according to IBM leadership, they never marry the brand identity to a single product. That would be shortsighted given the rapid change of technology, culture, and markets. Instead, they tend closely to the character of the organization. Being certain to stay true to the guiding principles defining that character. They understand it is the character of an organization that ultimately attracts or repels a given audience, a given constituency. Everything else is just detail.

Product is just detail. So are a host of other attributes that make up the experience any particular customer may have with a brand, be it service, design aesthetic, quality standards, distribution, marketing, or anything else. It's all detail. German-born American architect Ludwig Mies van der Rohe is noted to have said, "God is in the detail." And, in fact, it's in the detail that the customer experience resides. It must follow then that the minutia is a manifestation of the organization's character. This is, in essence, how and why great companies, great organizations, and great leaders attract followings, by manifesting purpose in the everyday experiences of their constituents (users). If it is transcendent purpose that customers attach themselves to, if it is the reason for being that ultimately defines an organization and its constituents, if it is Simon Sinek's "Why" that customers buy, then it naturally follows that guaranteeing these tenets are expressed at every point of interaction between a brand and a customer is the path to creating a following.

But it's more than just a following we want. We want loyalty, a long-term, sustainable relationship. From the perspective of a business, we want to sustain a buying relationship with our customers for the long-term. And we want those relationships to further new relationships. This is the foundation of growth. It's what fans of the NPI manage: customer satisfaction. The logic is that the greater the customer satisfaction within a given product or service category, the greater the likelihood of recommendation. The higher the rates of recommendation, the greater the likelihood for growth. If customers are satisfied to the degree they are willing to risk their social standing on recommending a product, brand, or service, then that product, brand, or service is providing a uniquely valuable proposition. And a uniquely valuable proposition means the user perceives that product, brand, or service to be the only one that can particularly meet their needs. Once that perception is struck, growth results, because when there is only one provider that uniquely services a particular point of view or need, all of those sharing that particular point of view or need have only one resource provider to turn to. This is when we see the rapid scaling of organizations, even in seemingly crowded categories. This is also the basis for long-term sustainable relationships. As long as the character of the organization is tended to deliberately, the manifestation in product and service will remain valuable, and it's here where brands have the opportunity to shape the stories that reside in the minds of their customers and in the stories shared in the marketplace, social media, and in recommendations among friends and family. The NPI simply measures a result: satisfaction. Our quest is to understand how satisfaction is happening at every single nuanced interaction, within every story associated with an organization, and how it resides at the heart of an organization's character.

Consider the stories that make up a brand's world, or universe. It's possible to organize all of the brand related stories into topics, subjects, and categories. These sorts of things fall under umbrellas related to product, service, and the general structure of a given organization. But as demonstrated, an organization's structure, product, and service are really manifested uniquely only when they are principle driven and the principles that drive the end-user experience are defined by the character or the company's reason for being—their core value, their purpose. The caveat at this juncture is to caution against thinking that this purpose is alluding to one's mission statement or strategic vision. This is absolutely not the case. The central core value held by an organization is the essential cause that motivated the founding. It is strictly the passion that was once the kernel of inspiration that formed the entity, that drove the organization of the thing into being in the first place.

Following this daisy chain from the kernel to the principles that organize the service, company, and product environments, and to the topics, subjects, and categories that are uniquely relevant to this brand, leads all the way to the actual stories that the user experiences. It's hopefully evident that this structure guarantees the end story is a reflection of the core value. The contrary is also true, that a single story experienced by a customer can be traced back to the founding principle at the center, the organization's reason for being. This I call the Story Universe.

The power of mapping an organization's story elements is that, if not mapped, the end user experience is potentially diluted, misinterpreted, or left to chance. Those brands that holistically understand their storytelling assure the right message is in the right place for the right customer at the right time. No customer experiences a brand in linear fashion, so manifesting the core value in every seemingly trivial user interaction assures the brand identity is clearly delineated. This clarity of communication is what begins to inspire a connection. This is the brand's Story Universe.

To create this architecture and to operationalize it is the job of the Customer Activation Cycle. In the case of a brand/customer relationship, the Customer Activation Cycle describes what is typically perceived as random and chaotic customer behavior, but actually predicts an outcome.

The Story Universe

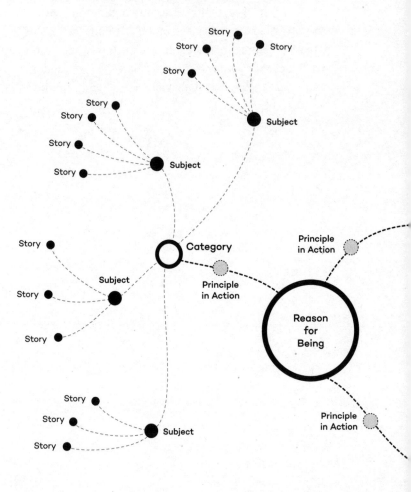

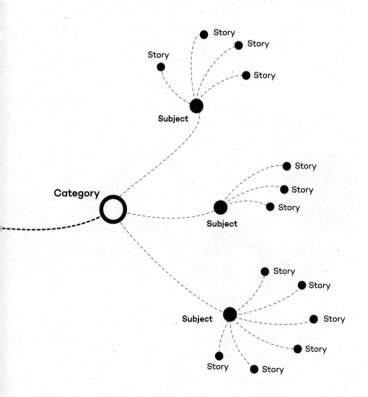

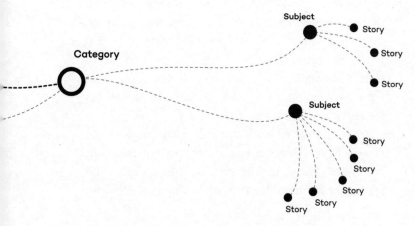

The Customer Activation Cycle

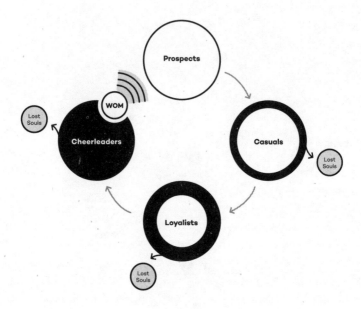

The Customer Activation Cycle provides the framework that shows how an individual evolves from an initial brand introduction to a point of advocacy. It also represents how loyalty itself happens because loyalty occurs in small, recurring instances that compound: patterns common among all customers that move them toward or away from long-term loyalty.

The basis of growth is to predictably cultivate and retain a population of customers who actively engage in the brand's image, purchase repeatedly over time, and spread the brand's value through recommendation and

Word of Mouth. The Customer Activation Cycle predicts why a customer will transact in response to what you do as a brand, and it predicts why that customer will continue to buy repeatedly over time or if that customer will not continue purchasing. It is the blueprint for turning casual customers into fans. Customer Activation is the process of deliberately creating brand champions.

The path from discovery to full Activation is marked by milestone information and/or experiences. The Customer Activation Cycle identifies each of these milestones: the first impression, testing and validating, deeper understanding, and finally alignment with core values. How this happens within the brand/customer relationship is unique to each brand. It acts as a logarithmic spiral, a template of growth, and once the pattern is known it is destined to continue indefinitely.

This process of Customer Activation in a brand environment begins with converting prospects. The largest segment by number, each individual represents only potential lifetime value per customer because they have yet to make a purchase of any kind. This segment, in standard marketing parlance, is the brand's target audience. Once a prospect makes a purchase, they become known as casuals. These customers have made at least one purchase. This group is a relatively large number in terms of customer count, but still nearly negligible in terms of lifetime value per customer. The primary goal is to retain these customers by validating their initial product and service expectations. The third stage in the process of Customer Activation is increased brand awareness. As the product and service experiences of these customers are broadened with multiple purchases and multiple brand interactions, greater brand knowledge is made possible. This stage is truly the most critical in developing long-term sustainable relationships because this is when and where these customers discern the principles upon which the brand operates. Unanimity of brand identity is indicative of third-stage customers. These customers are now known as loyalists. The final stage of Customer Activation is best described as aligning purpose. Cheerleaders agree with the purpose of the organization. The assumption of purpose is when and how individuals transcend their own boundaries by participating wholeheartedly in the identity and purpose of the organization, from which, because of its size, the individual feels a greater sense of impact. It is this transcendent purpose cheerleaders most relate to and uniquely identify with. The smallest in customer count, yet by far the highest lifetime value per customer, these customers represent the lifeblood of the brand customer base in terms of buying and recommending, or Word of Mouth. The main goal is to continually share the core value and reason for being in tangible ways with these customers. These are customers for life.

The brand and the individual embark on a journey, initiated by the customer, that culminates in agreement of purpose. Each customer must weave a path through the complexity of the totality of the brand landscape. Making that journey rewarding is a matter of putting the right information at the user's fingertips and creating the right experiences that move them along this progression of understanding such that they quickly and efficiently align along a set of core values. No customer engagement is the same, but each customer engagement requires the same key milestone bits of information, or brand experiences, to progress them along the path.

Guaranteeing this happens is the collective job of the Story Universe and the Customer Activation Cycle—our tools for architecting loyalty.

While customers experience a brand from the fringe to the center, ideally we can architect this experience from the center to the fringe. The progression to loyalty follows:

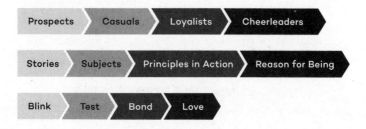

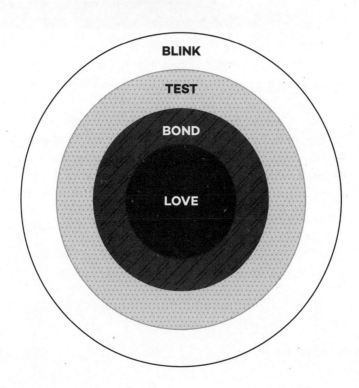

As powerful as this is from the perspectives of marketing and brand management, the breakthrough that the Customer Activation Cycle represents to the business world is in shifting our focus from measuring customer performance, just a single piece of the puzzle, to measuring repeatable behavior across the totality of brand performance. This is why the collective methodology of the Customer Activation Cycle and the Story Universe is the first and the only model that tracks the progression of a customer to advocacy by monetizing the qualitative attributes of brand identity.

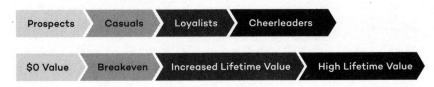

On average, practitioners realize a 40% to 70% increase in contribution dollars[v] over a 24 month period. For a 20-million-dollar business with five million dollars in contribution dollars, that translates into an additional two million dollars to $3.5 million. The strategic imperative for the organization from a profitability perspective is to create cheerleaders.

- Cheerleaders represent ten to twelve times the contribution dollars over first time buyers

- They advocate on your brand's behalf

- They are willing to pay premiums to remain with your brand

---

v   Aggregate from client work.

A new metric resides between each stage. It's called the Rate of Migration. It's where the art becomes science, where the qualitative is overlaid with the quantitative. This model marries the brand DNA to the distinct measurement of a customer's progression to a state of advocacy. This predictive algorithm takes chaos and creates order such that migration can be managed. And, by managing migration (Customer Activation) via the Customer Activation Cycle the entire idea of customer performance shifts from the traditional practices of monitoring the buying habits of the customer to ensuring each customer in each segment is getting the mission-critical information appropriate for their point in the progression.

Customers all have their own unique relationships with brands. But cheerleaders all share the same milestone experiences and information that triggered them to move from prospect to casual to loyalist to cheerleader.

It's foolhardy to bombard a prospect or casual with purpose when they are not even certain if they have an interest or faith in the product or service performance. It's equally wasteful to spend countless dollars promoting product features and benefits to loyalists and cheerleaders when they've already validated that the brand meets and exceeds those expectations. Simply put, prospects are attracted to style, casuals validate performance, loyalists align with beliefs, and cheerleaders transcend to purpose.

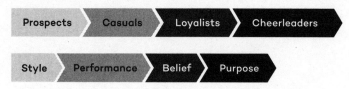

The result is advocacy. That's the goal. To constantly improve the rate at which a potential customer migrates to a state of advocacy.

With advocacy comes increased value over time, measured in both contribution dollars and recommendation rates. Cheerleaders are committed to the brand's product, service, company principles, and transcendent purpose. With that commitment comes the near unbreakable bond of brand advocacy. Love is great.

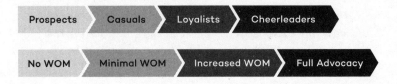

Prospects Casuals Loyalists Cheerleaders

No WOM Minimal WOM Increased WOM Full Advocacy

Long-term Sustainable Loyalty Defined in Terms of Value

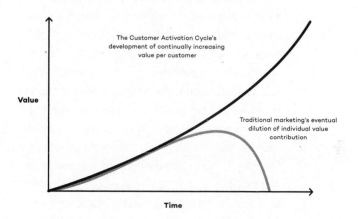

The Customer Activation Cycle's development of continually increasing value per customer

Value

Traditional marketing's eventual dilution of individual value contribution

Time

And so it goes; character defines, the definition is found in the detail, and it is the detail by which that user's wish, hope, and dream uniquely serve them based on their own narrowly defined needs, their own "natural frequency." Marketers do not create demand. Superior product does not always win the day. The lowest price does not always dictate outcome. And purchase frequency and recency do not define loyalty. In fact, what does win over and over again is aligned understanding, or resonance: an unspoken agreement between the provider and the user, where the provider creates its product or service based on a particular point of view, and the user is uniquely in need of that particular point of view and how it manifests in the end service or the end product.

> "We've never defined IBM by what we are selling. We've learned that at some point in the future, if you make that mistake you will have to go to a lot of expense and trouble to take out of people's hearts and minds that definition of IBM, because the punch card will have had its day, or the Selectric typewriter, or the mainframe, the PC, Watson, cloud, analytics, all those things. So, if we are not going to define our brand by what we make...what defines us? And it comes back to this notion of our corporate character, and that's our belief system, our purpose, and our mission, and what makes us Us. We tend to that and the brand takes care of itself."
>
> **JON IWATA**
> IBM SENIOR VICE PRESIDENT

This is the basis for long-term sustainable relationships. As long as the company's character is tended to deliberately, the manifestation in product and service will remain valuable. A first impression leads to validation of that first impression, which leads to deeper understanding and an alignment of beliefs: blink, test, bond, love. We move from a superficial introduction to a deep state of resonance.

The Progression of Resonance

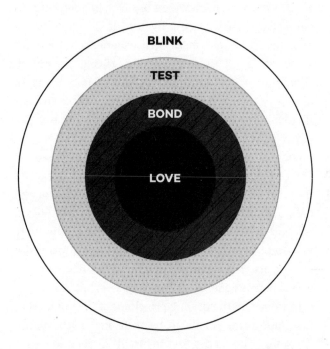

How does all of this really work in practice? First, think of the two models (the Customer Activation Cycle and the Story Universe) acting in concert, each their own visual model that together capture the invisible forces acting on the brand/customer relationship at every instance. The two perspectives create a visual of the patterns of behavior all of a brand's customers exhibit: good, bad, and indifferent. Second, imagine four little lightbulbs in the heads of those customers turning on one by one. One of my favorite clients of all time, an innovative company called Light & Motion, is a wonderful example of the power of these models. The company designs, manufacturers, sells, and services high-end personal lighting devices for diving, cycling, trekking, and more.

Light & Motion prospects are avid, lifelong outdoor enthusiasts. They place a high value on finely tuned equipment that enhances their experience of outdoor activities, be it surfing, cycling, diving, mountain climbing, or trail running. Of the myriad paths to discovery of Light & Motion, a prospect may see another rider at a bike race using a product, they may watch a video on YouTube about conscientious design, see the product in package at a local dive shop, or even see the Light & Motion van at a climbing event or festival. Each of these are initial, random touch points that tell a story all their own. This is the first impression, the shiny object. The job these random interactions do is simple: they make an impression and pull the prospect into a realm of curiosity, into a moment of infatuation. If architected well, when designed deliberately as an expression of the core value and the driving principles of the brand, that first impression will ideally be a reflection of the reason for being. This is the first lightbulb to click for these prospects: *Hmmm, that appeals to my particular point of view.*

Light & Motion casuals get to know what Integrated Design Engineering and Under One Roof mean to their overall product experience. These customers start to experience intimate details of the product that are telltale signs of the core value of the organization. They discover that the product performs uniquely because it seems to have been designed, engineered, and crafted in a conscientious manner. Little details emerge only upon experience of use. Overall, they begin to realize an enhanced experience of the product itself, and of their intended use of it. This is the second lightbulb to turn on in their heads: *Hmmm, this product performs uniquely because it seems to have been designed and engineered differently.*

When lightbulb number two turns on, this customer takes another step toward becoming a lifelong fan of Light & Motion.

As this relationship percolates, our prospect that has become a casual is now on the verge of becoming a loyalist. Another purchase or two, another customer service experience or two, a few more visits to the company Web site, or an additional visit to the local outdoor store all provide further and further texture highlighting the principles driving the organization as a whole. These principles include company policies and structure, product design and quality, and the service environment. At this level of discovery, our casual-turned-loyalist has further unearthed some of the organizing principles of this specific company, including the principle of Under One Roof. Under One Roof is exactly what it sounds like: the entirety of the company is housed under one roof in one facility in Marina, California. From design and engineering, to manufacturing, to customer service, it's all in one place. When a customer calls with a problem, that issue is not just dealt with by some customer service dictate, the answer actually resides only a few footsteps from its origin. If a switch malfunction is the problem, engineering or production can chime in on the issue directly and either elect to remedy the problem with a quick fix, a replacement, or a refund. If it's a recurring problem, the entire production process can be alerted and the product improved literally on the spot. This is one aspect of why the quality level at Light & Motion is so high, because beyond their own field-testing, they also have an immediate feedback loop built into the organization as a whole. This is truly conscientious design, an organizing principle of the company. Fans of good design, and well-wrought thinking like this, come to favor Light & Motion as this level of intimacy is experienced. Our loyalist is now a very big fan. The third lightbulb clicks on.

The final lightbulb for our soon-to-be lifelong customer is the discovery of Light & Motion's core founding value, the passion that drives the company from its deepest root. Light & Motion's "Why" is the belief in questioning everything and challenging the status quo to continuously improving the experience of life—this, in fact, being the reason all the rest exists, why they make the product they do, why they design and engineer it with a philosophy of Integrated Design Engineering, why they house everything under one roof, why they practice an absolute customer satisfaction service philosophy and on and on. For cheerleaders, this is music to their ears. They, too, question everything, demand innovation that ensures the least environmental impact, and ultimately are out to experience the outdoors in the most real and connected way they can. Light & Motion is a partner in that endeavor and as such, these cheerleaders that gain this level of understanding consider Light & Motion their partner. As long as Light & Motion stays true to that core value, these customers will remain customers for life. The fourth and final lightbulb illuminates.

Now we see the fully activated customer. As our prospect first discovered Light & Motion, they initially discovered Stories. Then, as the prospect became a casual, they discovered the Principles behind the product and service. Then, as that casual matriculated to become a loyalist, the discovery of company principles came to their understanding. And, finally, our customer's journey concludes at their ultimate destination as a cheerleader unearthing the founding core value of the organization. The Activation of this customer was a journey from the fringes of the Story Universe to the center of the Story Universe.

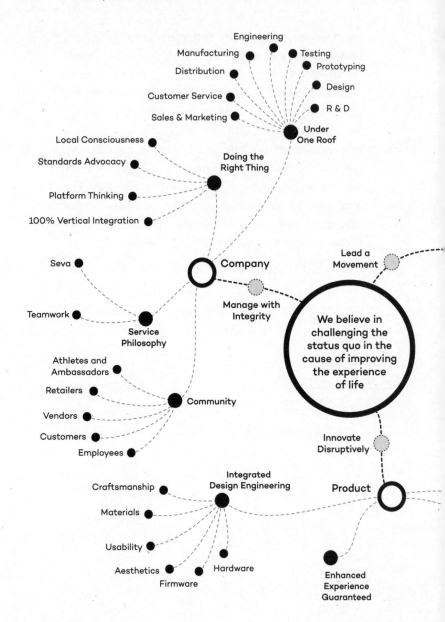

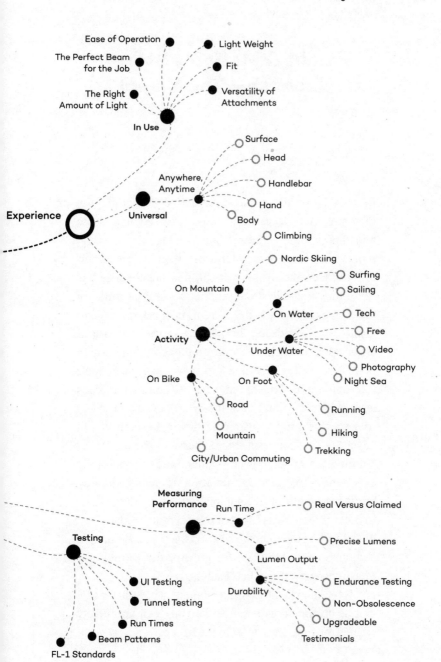

Ease of Operation

The Perfect Beam
for the Job

The Right
Amount of Light

In Use

Light Weight

Fit

Versatility of
Attachments

Experience

Universal

Anywhere,
Anytime

Surface

Head

Handlebar

Hand

Body

Activity

On Mountain

Climbing

Nordic Skiing

On Water

Surfing

Sailing

Under Water

Tech

Free

Video

Photography

Night Sea

On Bike

On Foot

Road

Mountain

City/Urban Commuting

Running

Hiking

Trekking

Testing

Measuring
Performance

Run Time

Real Versus Claimed

Lumen Output

Precise Lumens

Durability

Endurance Testing

Non-Obsolescence

Upgradeable

Testimonials

UI Testing

Tunnel Testing

Run Times

Beam Patterns

FL-1 Standards

Light & Motion's Story Universe—The Visual

In order for this to be a predictive algorithm, the Customer Activation Cycle must take seeming chaos and make order. The Story Universe is a visual representation of that order. Customers all have their own unique relationships with brands, but cheerleaders share the same milestone experiences and information that triggered them to move from prospect to casual to loyalist to cheerleader. By asking a series of questions of representative cheerleaders and listening intently to them describe their relationship, their experiences, their interpretations of the brand, a host of common threads emerge. A mere handful of interviews uncover the key triggers that propel customers down the path of full advocacy. The common threads serve as the fodder for defining the needs of each segment and the milestone experiences that lead to migration at each stage. Any brand's strength of developing advocacy resides here, in the truth told by existing or representative advocates. Revisiting the Customer Activation Cycle in this example demonstrates a template for growth, the formula for repeatedly activating cheerleaders.

Here, now, is the exciting moment. The architecture of the customer experience can be seen intuitively emanating from the center to the fringe.

The first and most important driving force of every single story that every customer can potentially experience, be they a prospect, casual, loyalist, or cheerleader, is a direct result, manifestation, or outcome of the core value at the center.

The core value is made manifest in the principles of company, product, and service. Those become Stories that are ultimately the tangible experiences of the customer. This customer experience is literally designed and architected to ensure every customer that holds the same core beliefs will progress over time to become a cheerleader.

A simple story here hopefully illustrates the beauty of the model in practice. Engineering at Light & Motion is not driven by the marketplace, or by sales projections, it's really driven by a passion for solving problems. Our story involves a rabid bike commuter that suffered through five years of commuting in the harsh winters of rural Germany and urban commutes in Seattle, who eventually needed to address the deteriorating performance of his five-year-old Stella 300 Dual headlights. After a few correspondences with the Light & Motion service rep, the decision was made to send the suspect lights to Light & Motion for some diagnostics. Although the warranty had expired three years prior, and Light & Motion no longer produced this particular design, the team at Light & Motion, dedicated to an "enhanced experience of life," elected to fully rebuild the lights, replacing the cables and bulbs, and servicing the casing and gaskets. When the lights arrived back to the customer's doorstep, he was ecstatic to have gotten a new lease on the life of his product. It would be a mistake to misclassify this as a classic over-deliver customer service story, but paying close attention, we see the core value of the organization manifesting in a single event played out between a customer service rep, a customer, and the product team at Light & Motion—a decision that overrides the dictates of the written, public warranty, without the need for querying management. A clear manifestation of principle creating a one of a kind experience.

Light & Motion's principle is simple: first see the problem, then create a solution for it. In the personal lighting world, that means first and foremost enabling an outdoor experience in a poorly lit space, whether that's underwater, on the side of a mountain, or on a dark city street. Regardless of the circumstance, it's about the physical attributes of a product enhancing the experience of the activity. In the Light & Motion Story Universe, this is then a shared value that must be captured in some form of story. In this case, it certainly manifests in the product. It's also in the shared love of sport, and in how Light & Motion speaks to the experience of the outdoors. It's also found in the conscientious design philosophy and, as example, it can even be found written into the particular language of the warranty:

"OUR ENHANCED EXPERIENCE GUARANTEE

We built it here in California and we will replace, repair, or upgrade it for the life of the product. Our two-year warranty doesn't merely provide you with peace of mind—it begins a conversation: about our commitment to you as a fellow outdoor enthusiast and as a good human being. When you get a Light & Motion product, you also inherit our relentless pursuit of an enhanced experience, the perfect light."

The warranty is a story in the schema of the Story Universe, its effect on progressing customers to advocacy, tangible.

Light & Motion's CEO, Daniel Emerson, speaks to the idea that product integrity reflects the organization that creates it when quoting professor Kim Clark: "The [product] is an artifact that represents the effort and creativity of every individual that contributed to its creation and production." This eloquently aligns with how Light & Motion cheerleaders see the products that reside in their lives on whole.

"I have a personal connection to the company that you can't market...I am at fault for the amount of things I have...it's not about spending money, it's about creating a connection. I just sold a nineteen sixty-eight Porsche that I bought in nineteen seventy-eight. I finally sold it and found the right home for it. Something that cares for me I find a connection with it. [I have a pair of] nineteen seventy-four Tiger shoes that I played volleyball in, and I know that these things provide a connection. And although these things are inanimate, they have earned my respect."

LIGHT & MOTION CUSTOMER

**"Why so many predictions
fail—but some don't: we focus
on what is easiest to measure
rather
than on what is important."**

NATE SILVER, *THE SIGNAL AND THE NOISE*

CHAPTER FIVE

DESIGNING AND ARCHITECTING LOYALTY:

Exploring Purposeful Connection

The Brand Ecosystem, and the process of understanding the relationship between character and detail, is essential to creating lifelong customers. Helping customers relate to character in every interaction, helping them see a company's authenticity at every stage, and helping them relate to their own character and set of values helps develop what we'll call Behavioral Loyalty— loyalty based on shared values and understanding.

How character manifests in the detail, within the end product or service that the user interacts with and in the overall brand and service environment that the user interacts with showcases unique experiences. The end results are the artifacts of the organization's character.

Transcendent Purpose

Daniel Pink has written extensively about what motivates us in the workplace, at home, and in school. In his 2009 book *Drive*, Pink cites four decades of research proving that human beings perform best and experience the greatest satisfaction when: 1) We are in control of our own lives, 2) We learn, create and master new things, and 3) We contribute to improving the world. In simpler terms it is autonomy, mastery, and purpose that together drive satisfaction. What is most relevant and supportive of our observations in the world of loyalty is Daniel Pink's revelation that people feel the greatest satisfaction when we find a means "to do better by ourselves and our world." When I look back on my personal and professional life, I see that it is a constant struggle and process to live a life of autonomy, mastery, and purpose—and while I know the value, it takes daily commitment to remember.

One summer when I was ten years old, I learned to sail. My parents had enrolled me in a city-run recreational beginning sailing class, a two-week course that met every morning that summer for three hours. I remember stepping into one of the eight-foot-long Sabots and sailing away from the dock with little hesitation. While most of the other kids bumped into things, spun in circles somewhat out of control, and worked on learning the basics, sailing came entirely intuitively to me. I began venturing away, sailing upwind, downwind, pretty much anywhere and everywhere I wanted to go. In the harbor that summer, the water separated me from everything and everyone else. The sounds were entirely unique to my experience. The pressure of the sail and the tug on the tiller connected me to the wind and the water.

Sailing was intimately tied to things purely of nature. The feel of the ocean and the wind through the physical boat consumed me. The connection to the environment transported me. It was transcendent. I truly believe my first moments sailing were also the first experiences I had communing with nature in a way that was meaningful, and hence the moment I began to develop my own values separate from my parents and my peers.

By the time I'd entered the University of California, Irvine as a freshman, my passion for sailing had only grown. I spent countless hours sitting in the library reading articles in sailing magazines and books on sailing around the world. Sailing made me feel whole in a way unlike anything else in my life. Although I didn't know why, I trusted it and devoted virtually all of my attention to learning more.

At this point, I was on the water five days a week. Three days of small boat practice per week with the UC Irvine Varsity Sailing Team, and both weekend days either sailing boats offshore to the Channel Islands or Mexico, or competing for the team inshore at small boat events up and down the coast. I encountered storms, crazy threatening waves, and days of perfect calm. The physical experience of sailing is in many ways painful. It's cold, wet, noisy, and physically exhausting. It's hard on your skin, eyes, hands, shoulders, and back. I sailed so much during my college days that I had permanent open cuts on my fingers from chafe and wear that even tape and gloves couldn't prevent or assist in healing. None of that mattered, my near-daily meditation on the water was the only thing that did. I took the lessons of meditation I learned from being on the water and began studying Buddhism. Alan Watts and other authors captured the essence of what I was experiencing, disappearing into the fluid mediums of air and water.

The values that I discovered during those first sailing years have become lifelong values. And it was during this time of discovery that Patagonia and its products became more and more a part of my world. My esoteric pastime didn't warrant crazy-expensive gear, though as my experiences took me further and further into harsh conditions of saltwater and cold, it became increasingly important to dress appropriately (even though I couldn't afford it). I came across my first real Patagonia product by chance—a rust-colored fleece jacket overlooked somehow in the team lost and found. Nobody claimed it for weeks, so it went to me—the first taker. It was stiff, and a bit scratchy, but a perfect fit. I wore it incessantly: to school, offshore, inshore, pre-sail, post-sail. It went everywhere with me. It pulled moisture away from my skin, dried within minutes, blocked cold, cut wind, and easily took the litany of abuses to its stitching and fabrication. It's the only piece of clothing I remember from my days as a college student and sailor.

During that time, once a year, my dreamscape of sailing and the ocean included studying the Patagonia catalog. In the early days at Patagonia, they produced a catalog that was more of an annual coffee table book than a direct-to-consumer mailing. It was part of the outdoor enthusiast's library. At least, it was definitely part of mine. It spoke my language. The imagery, the stories, the products, and the philosophy resonated with me unlike any other product company. It wasn't really about the technical features and benefits, although those things were present, I'd already become a fanatical product follower because of my singular rust-colored fleece jacket. The annual book illustrated that impossible experiences are possible and that a higher purpose drove the organization's actions. Patagonia spoke of a reverence for nature that none that I knew of had expressed previously, and they did it with simple, powerful photography and storytelling about people living wholly in their passion: stories of adventurers climbing faraway mountains, skiers traversing unknown slopes, and sailors exploring the most remote oceans. I formed a bond with these beliefs. Instead of graduating and entering the workforce soon enough to be financially well-endowed such that I could afford Patagonia gear, I took the path of most resistance and accepted a job as a sailmaker, and eventually a sailing coach, all really to further my ability to be on the water at every opportunity. Instead of the catalog spurring me to buy more gear, it inspired me to delve deeper into the life of the dirtbag. In Patagonia parlance, dirtbag is a term of reverence describing the individual that commits every ounce of their life to their passion for the outdoors, eschewing most cultural norms. In my case, I poured everything into my love of the ocean and sailing.

In 1998, I found out about an open position at Patagonia as head of product and marketing for Patagonia Sailing. The position had been open for some time, and it appeared as though they had likely filled it. I wrote an email, not about my qualifications but about my beliefs. It was about why I was moved by the values of the organization and why I felt it was more a calling than a job. I attached two resumes: my business and education in one, and my sailing experiences in the other. I signed the email: "I'm a surfer, swimmer, sailor, vegetarian, yoga-doing, ocean-traveling, bike-commuting Alan Watts-reading dirtbag that buys organic cloth diapers for our young children, that's dreamed of working at Patagonia for a decade." Somehow I knew the people at Patagonia hired based on belief rather than on acumen and if I could impart just a gist of what I practiced, they'd give me a shot.

My first day at work in a "real" job at Patagonia was in April 1998, and for the next eight years I evolved as a contributor to the Patagonia brand.

That evolution proved to be fast and furious. My original responsibility at Patagonia was to find a path of growth for the line of sailing product, for Patagonia as a brand in the global sailing community. In week one, the person that hired me left the company, summarily exited. My new boss was less the nurturing kind. A few months later, I was also almost summarily dismissed. It was made clear that I needed to learn how Patagonia operated because nothing at Patagonia was done the way the rest of the world did things. Then came the learning curve. I abandoned everything I knew or thought I knew about marketing and branding. I started anew by studying the historical milestones that contributed to periods of growth of the company. I'd done this homework before, but this time I looked specifically for the organizing principle that was driving the milestone decisions. Rather than looking at the decisions themselves, the circumstances surrounding them, or even the outcome, I looked to see the underlying purpose.

After a tumultuous, yet relatively short, nine months into my tenure as the sailing marketer, upon my advice, the Board of Directors elected to end production of high-end outerwear for sailing. With that decision, my job was eliminated and I was again effectively summarily dismissed. I was briefly a lame duck, but soon landed in what it seems now was my destined position at Patagonia: as head of the fledgling e-commerce business. In the early spring of 1999, I was put in charge of myself and one other employee. We were the Internet Group. The next seven years, from 1999 to 2006, Patagonia and I were to change dramatically, and central to that change was the discovery of how customers of Patagonia, people like me, became ardent champions of the brand and the cause and how they come to conclude "clothing can have a soul."

My sailing story and employee relationship with Patagonia highlights how my values connected me to Patagonia's character and details. It's not a unique story. Patagonia's customers report this kind of interaction all the time. It's the larger context created by the founding principles that draws people to the front door and keeps them coming back year after year. There's a palpable reality that the cause is a shared responsibility and that we are all in it together, making an impact. Those who have interacted with the company frequently enough and in enough varying ways have gleaned what goes on behind the scenes. Those that have proven to themselves that what they suspect is true, or hope is true, is actually true. This experience being in the trenches of the direct business at Patagonia was my first eyewitness account of the power of purpose. Reading Daniel Pink's work years later validated what I'd seen firsthand time and again at Patagonia and come to study qualitatively and quantitatively through Patagonia's direct-to-consumer business.

"Customers become advocates of brands because they develop an emotional connection with their core purpose. Brands that elicit advocacy provide a value beyond just product quality and experience. This connection is something that deserves analysis, as it is the foundation of true loyalty."

MICHAEL CROOKE[vi]
PhD, FORMER PATAGONIA CEO

This thread has been touched on by several people: Kim Clark, speaking about product as an artifact that is representative of the people that create it, Jon Iwata describing character rather than just product as a means to define an organization, and Michael Crooke noting advocacy results when users experience value beyond product quality and experience. This is where the distinction between one provider and the next resides.

Seeing is Believing

This manifests absolutely in the examination of customer attributes. The example below demonstrates the distinction of the qualitative attributes of a Patagonia casual customer and a Patagonia advocate:

---

vi   Michael Crooke and Craig Wilson, "Creating Advocates: A Values-Oriented
Approach to Developing Brand Loyalty," *Graziado Business Review*, gbr.pepperdine
.edu/2011/09/creating-advocates-a-values-oriented-approach-to-develop-
ing-brand-loyalty/

Advocate	Customers	Casual
High Quality	Impressions of Patagonia	High Quality
Many thousands	Lifetime spend	Many tens
Many per year	Recommendations	None per year
Yes	Family wears Patagonia?	No
Yes	Surrounded by people with Patagonia?	No
Yes	Outdoor experience with Patagonia?	No
Yes	Can a piece of clothing have a soul?	No
Yes	Ironclad experience	No

Kazaks, Alex, and Ayr Muir-Harmony. Customer Life Cycle Study.

Patagonia, 2004.

Daniel Pink notes in *Drive* that "people want to be part of something bigger than themselves, to help achieve something that they can't necessarily achieve on their own." Customers see their association with authenticity in brands the same way. They see this association as a way to make their world a little bit better. Therefore, cultivating customer loyalty is a matter of establishing a blueprint for delivering clearly demarcated experiences and communications across every single channel, and at every touch point. These experiences are based specifically on core purpose. This is the practice of architecting loyalty.

> "Spending an inordinate amount of time and money on your sign, or your jingle, or your Web site is beside the point. It's *every* point of contact that matters. If you're not consistent and authentic, the timing of that first impression is too hard to predict to make it worth the journey. On the other hand, if you can cover all the possible impressions and allow the consumer to make them into a coherent story, you win."
>
> **SETH GODIN**
> *ALL MARKETERS ARE LIARS*

It follows then that the effort to craft the communications and the experiences is a holistic undertaking, architecting the brand's core values into the landscape of every touch point of branding, marketing, product, and service. Similar to the blueprint for a home, it's the beginning of everything.

> "A maniacal dedication to authentic purpose is what separates the strong from the weak

in the competitive brand landscape. A great brand has depth. If one digs into the details of an exceptional organization, it is evident that the espoused values drive the sustainable competitive advantage.

"Whatever one does should be done thoroughly, that is the crux of connecting the values of the brand with the values of the consumer."

MICHEAL CROOKE[vii]

PhD AND FORMER CEO AT PATAGONIA:

Whole Foods is an example of an organization with a big idea that is tied directly to the minutia:

"We are building a business in which high standards permeate all aspects of our company. Quality is a state of mind at Whole Foods Market. Our motto—Whole Foods, Whole People, Whole Planet."

There is clearly a drive to extend their mission into every single activity in their value chain:

"Our Vision Statement reflects the hopes and intentions of many people. We do not believe it always accurately portrays the way things currently are at Whole Foods Market so much as the way we would like things to be. It is our dissatisfaction with the current reality, when compared with what is possible, that spurs us toward excellence and toward creating a better person, company, and world. When Whole

---

vii   Ibid.

Foods Market fails to measure up to its stated Vision, as it inevitably will at times, we should not despair. Rather let us take up the challenge together to bring our reality closer to our vision. The future we will experience tomorrow is created one step at a time today."

Customers interact with brands in remarkably minute ways, interfacing with a single customer service agent over the phone, receiving a package in the mail, or walking by a storefront display. In the case of Whole Foods, a display of hopefully ripe and tasty organic produce. The defining moments of success of any brand occur under a microscope.

How then does one attend to every detail? By mapping them, as we have seen. The technique is to employ the Story Universe and the Customer Activation Cycle and map every interaction and possible interaction in tedious detail. It sounds mundane, but the exercise that is most useful to assure every nuance is accounted for is creating flow charts of the customer's journey through the brand landscape. Every possible touch point should be identified, and the appropriate experience, communication, or piece of information should be detailed—like a great restaurateur polishing every glass, garnishing every dish in exquisite form, and attending to each and every subtle need of their guests.

The quest is not to imagine some linear pathway that any given customer might travel. The quest is to be certain that no matter what interaction they have along their chosen path, the right experience, the right message, the right information is at their fingertips. By mapping the experience comprehensively, you'll discover where the breakdowns occur so you can enact a remedy. It's the only way to be certain your customers are getting the totality of the experience you feel is truly the most important, the entirety of the experience defined in the Customer Activation Cycle and the stories captured in the Story Universe.

This exercise goes downstream to users and upstream through the supply chain. If the product and its development process does not reflect the brand's core values, the user will know.

A user's experiences interacting with a brand at various times and various touch points leads them to understand what it is the brand truly stands for. Winning customers is about meeting the basic expectations and seeing things eye-to-eye. Once every touch point is mapped, apply your particular point of view to every one of them. Walk through every scenario. The digital industry spends endless dollars on usability testing, persuasion design, and mapping tasks to flow charts. The retail industry has their customer flow diagrams. Mapping every aspect of the value chain and crafting the entirety of the user's experience specifically to reflect the core values comprehensively solidifies your brand in the consumer's mind.

Architecting loyalty must be the new discipline required in the brand creation and development process.

What we've learned so far is that companies like Patagonia and Whole Foods transform their customers into passionate Brand Advocates. We've reviewed in concept how they do it, and how they "create such strong affection for their brands that their customers are compelled to become active brand champions." We've also learned that it's not lightning in a bottle, that the phenomenon is a matter of clearly aligning commonly held values with the user. This is the secret that strategically and tactically turns average customers into Brand Advocate superheroes.

These superheroes, or cheerleaders, represent the asset that contributes the lion's share of profit contribution to the organization as a whole. In turn, we know that loyal customer behavior is ultimately the only thing that drives growth, profitability, and guarantees long-term value. Architecting loyalty then is paramount to an organization's success.

If long-term sustainability isn't argument enough, these superhero customers represent more value in terms of recruitment, i.e., advocacy. These customers are described as cheerleaders, because they actively engage to promote the brands, products, services, and causes they believe in to wide circles of people. These are the mechanics of building a following, architecting a willing following of Brand Advocates. It's this following that exponentially grows businesses and grows the bottom line.

> "Word of Mouth is the most efficient form of branding, marketing, advertising, and selling. Brand Advocates are the most powerful medium. Arming the Brand Advocate then with a 'highly repeatable' thought is the ultimate campaign strategy."
>
> **LEE GOLDSTEIN**
> DIGO BRANDS

"Ninety-two percent of people trust recommendations from friends and family above all other forms of advertising when making a purchasing decision."

DAVID MIELACH[viii]
BUSINESS NEWS DAILY

The end game is to create and inspire Brand Advocates and deploy highly repeatable thoughts which create, inspire, and maintain Brand Advocates. Multiplying their effectiveness on behalf of your brand builds scale in the fastest, most efficient way possible.

Ultimately, this is where long-term value resides. Profitability is a function of loyalty. According to Fred Reichheld, founder of Bain & Company's loyalty practice and the author of *The Loyalty Effect: The Hidden Force Behind Growth*: 1) A typical company receives roughly 56% of its business from existing customers; 2) More than 50% of customers are willing to pay a 20% to 25% premium for their favorite brand before switching to another; 3) In some categories, a five percent increase in loyal customers can produce a 95% increase in profitability; 4) In certain luxury categories, ten percent of the customers generate 50% of the sales.

In summary, advocates are worth their weight in gold. They drive growth and profitability by making recommendations, paying premium prices, and costing less to reach via marketing.

viii   David Mielach, "Why Word of Mouth Trumps Traditional Advertising," *Business News Daily*, April 13, 2012. www.businessnewsdaily.com/2353-consumer-ad-trust.html

The Loyalty Effect on Profit[ix]

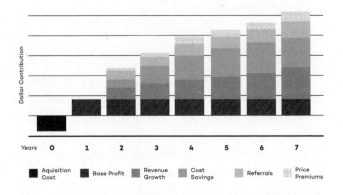

A sobering fact, however, is that the average company loses between ten percent and 30% of its customers each year. The good news is just a five percent reduction in customer defection rates can increase profits by 25% to 80%. Satisfying and retaining current customers is three to ten times cheaper than acquiring new customers.

With all of this said, according to the American Management Association, 75% of the time that customers defect from brands, it's due to shortcomings in the user experience.

Reducing defection by remedying shortcomings in the user experience is most effective if the user experience is a reflection of core purpose. Advocates operate based on adopting the founding principle of an organization. It's

---

ix   "The Loyalty Effect on Profit," Fred Reichheld, *The Loyalty Effect.*

their inspiration. Therefore, architecting user experiences that clearly reflect the founding passion of the organization is paramount.

In late 2008, I collaborated on a consulting project with Rich Hill and we were attempting to explain this phenomenon by using examples of how some companies we'd witnessed scaled in their early years. How was it that founders of garage band-like brands gained a following that then attracted more followers, and eventually found their brands serving a large audience of buyers? What was the progression, what was the secret to these self-starter brands that built upon the passion of the founding vision and scaled largely on Word of Mouth to become relatively large entities serving relatively diverse customers? Rich grabbed a piece of paper. He started with a seed that represented the founders bright idea, the kernel. Then he drew a concentric circle around the center that represented the first customers to respond to the idea: most likely the founder's friends and family, but also the early movers, the people that were insiders and got news of the idea first. Those were the early adopters. Then he drew one more concentric circle and that represented "everyone else," the audience en masse. These customers are pure followers, relying on the first, core group of buyers to take the early risk and establish credibility of the brand. That model is alive and well today. We call it "The Kernel."

Visualizing Customer Types

Founding Vision: This is why you are in business, the founding principle that your most loyal customers fall in love with. Not your product, but the passion behind the product, your reason for being, your transcendent purpose. This is The Kernel.

Core Users: These are the "professionals," the customers that are fully versed in the product, service, or lifestyle. They live it every day. These customers define your brand.

Dog Walkers: This is the largest group of customers. They are made up of followers, posers, and wannabes. They make up the majority of unit sales, and they buy ancillary product, but they are not the audience you have in mind when you design your product or service.

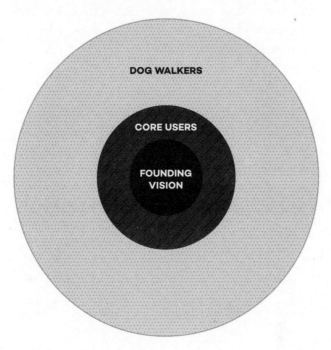

Risk: Because there are large unit sales to be had within the dog walker category, often brand managers and merchandisers will chase this group's dollars by designing product just for them. This is proven to be the beginning of brand erosion and the death of loyalty. Brands scale based on innovators and early adopters leading the charge. The early majority and late majority people only buy after 11% to 16% market share has been realized.

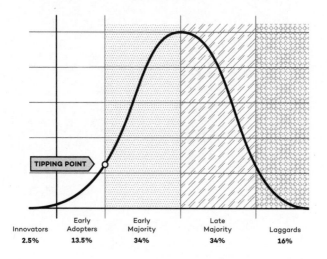

Innovators	Early Adopters	Early Majority	Late Majority	Laggards
2.5%	13.5%	34%	34%	16%

This phenomenon was made famous by Malcolm Gladwell in his book *The Tipping Point,* but also reiterated by Simon Sinek in *Start With Why*. It is also worthy of a revisit in the context of loyalty, because it so well demonstrates not so much how trends progress and evolve into popular culture, but rather, in this instance, it's demonstrative of how trends within loyalty can die.

Once a brand moves from its core purpose, core users will drop the brand. Dog walkers are, by design, followers. If there is no one to follow (i.e., the core users), the dog walkers will eventually fade as well.

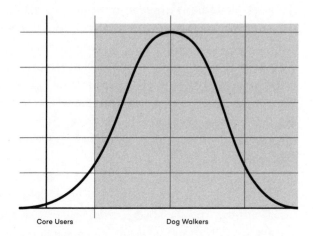

Core Users   Dog Walkers

Case in point is the rise and fall of Eddie Bauer. Eddie Bauer was founded in 1920. It offered a full range of expedition gear, goose down, and specialized in outdoor gear.

> "Eddie Bauer's original products were created out of necessity rather than style. These great accomplishments came straight from the heart of a man with big ideas."

> **KURT CLARK**[x]
> *SEATTLE POST-INTELLIGENCER*

Innovation was a significant part of those big ideas. Eddie Bauer created the first down jacket in

x   Kurt Clark, "90 Years of Eddie Bauer History On Display in Bellevue," *Seattle Post-Intelligencer*, July 7, 2010. blog.seattlepi.com/bellev-ue-pi/2010/07/07/90-years-of-eddie-bauer-history-on-display-in-bellevue/

1936, the first down flight suit in 1942, and the first mountaineering parka in 1953. A love of the outdoors, and an untamable spirit of adventure, drove the brand's character. Along the way, the core principles of designing and manufacturing rugged expedition-grade gear for serious outdoor pursuits waned in favor of chasing the dog walkers, the milestone coming with the sale of Eddie Bauer to General Mills in 1971. With this sale began a long line of events eroding the founding vision: retail expansion into malls rather than staying strictly with specialty outdoor retailers. Slow moving merchandise like sleeping bags, tents, and fishing equipment were replaced with street wear for men and women. The brand shifted focus from "expedition outfitter" to "active casual outfitter" merchandising, catering to the seventy percent of retail buyers that were women, and licensing deals struck in categories entirely tangential to the core outdoor market, including eyewear, furniture, bicycles, and automobiles.

The dog walkers were being pursued on all fronts, while the core users all but abandoned.

> "Two years ago our brand stumbled. We used trendy colors on classic clothes. It was a mistake. We got distracted and tried to reach too many segments."
>
> **JULIE RODWAY**
> EVP OF MERCHANDISING, EDDIE BAUER

Juxtaposing the trajectories of Eddie Bauer and Patagonia is a telling exercise.

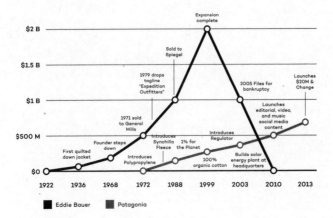

Patagonia, on the other hand, stayed their course adhering to their core principles.

> "Every time I've done the right thing for the environment, I've made a profit."
>
> **YVON CHOUINARD**

We have seen how connecting a company's core purpose with customers' core purpose leads to business success and how losing your focus by chasing the dog walkers can lead to loss of customers and reduced profit. Now we need to understand what makes our best customers tick, and it's not always what we assume.

"Everything that can be counted does not necessarily count; everything that counts cannot necessarily be counted."

ALBERT EINSTEIN

CHAPTER SIX

Throwing the Baby Out with the Bath Water

The idea of staying true to your core principles and relating well to your core users makes sense when viewed in the context of The Kernel model. The Eddie Bauer example helps prove the point. Late adopters follow early adopters, consequently, having no early adopters (no core) means having no followers. What's dumbfounding is that the mistake of ignoring this principle is often the result of rational data steering us to the wrong conclusions, not because we aren't naturally smart beings, but rather because, in certain circumstances, and faced with overwhelmingly obvious quantitative data, our qualitative mind overrides our rational thinking. In other words, we make gut calls and then justify them with rational thinking. With the Eddie Bauer example, it was the pursuit of the dog walkers that appeared to be intuitively the right thing to do, when in fact it was the reputation built as an expedition outfitter that appealed to the core users and those core users pull along the fringe. The manager's intuition, to cater to the larger slice of revenue the seventy percent of women's retail buyers represented, lead them to believe success resided with what was the lion's share of their customers. The rational mind then supported that decision with comparative numbers, all the while ignoring the phenomenon of *The Tipping Point* and what brought them success in the first place.

The very first data we as humans relied on came in the form of stories. Our brains are hard wired for story, much less so for rational data. Put simply, we're vulnerable to anecdotes that mislead or present false conclusions unsupported by data.

Kahneman is a psychologist and Nobel laureate. His Nobel was awarded in 2002 for the work he and Tversky (Tversky's Nobel was awarded posthumously) created on the psychology of judgment and decision-making. Together they developed "the cognitive basis for human errors" back in 1973. Kahneman's book, *Thinking, Fast and Slow*, explains in great detail, among other things, why humans err in the face of seemingly clear logic.

Consider The Linda Problem, what Kahneman calls the "best-known and most controversial" of he and Tversky's experiments:

> "Participants in the experiment were told about an imaginary young woman named Linda, who is single, outspoken, and very bright, and who, as a student, was deeply concerned with issues of discrimination and social justice. The participants were then asked which was more probable: (1) Linda is a bank teller, or (2) Linda is a bank teller and is active in the feminist movement. The overwhelming response was that (2) was more probable. In other words, given the background information furnished, 'feminist bank teller' was more likely than 'bank teller.' This is, of course, a blatant violation of the laws of probability. (Every feminist bank teller is a bank teller; adding

a detail can only lower the probability.) Yet even among students in Stanford's Graduate School of Business, who had extensive training in probability, eighty-five percent flunked the Linda problem. One student, when informed that she had committed an elementary logical blunder, responded, 'I thought you just asked for my opinion.'"

JIM HOLT[xi]
THE NEW YORK TIMES

What has gone wrong here? An easy question (How coherent is the narrative?) is substituted for a more difficult one (How probable is it?). And this, according to Kahneman, is the source of many of the biases that infect our thinking. We jump to an intuitive conclusion based on a "heuristic"—an easy but imperfect way of answering hard questions—and then our more lazy, rational mind endorses this heuristic answer without bothering to scrutinize its logic.

Marketers have a Linda Problem. Profitability resides with our best customers. They buy the most. They buy more frequently. They even buy our premium-priced product. Because of this, we begin to tell ourselves a narrative about our best customers that ignores the underlying rational reality that our best customers became that way through a rather elaborate process. We also intuitively conclude they are preferred customers, preferred over all other customers, and should be managed accordingly. The truth is that our best customers are our core customers, and our most

xi   Jim Holt, "Two Brains Running," *The New York Times*, November 25, 2011. www.nytimes.com/2011/11/27/books/review/thinking-fast-and-slow-by-dan-iel-kahneman
-book-review.html?_r=0

valuable customers have gone through an elaborate process to understand what makes those core customers tick, what lies at the center of The Kernel, what is the founding principle. They've lived through the process of getting to know us, and through that process we've satisfied them. They are happy, and they are buying accordingly. Our collective Linda Problem is that the vast majority of our customers, including prospects, casuals, and even loyalists, have yet to become our best customers (cheerleaders) and are possibly not-so-satisfied just yet. By ignoring the potential of all of our "not necessarily best customers yet," we are ignoring what these segments represent to the future value of our organization. We leave lots of money on the table because, as we've seen in the Customer Activation Cycle model, there is a high likelihood that until a customer reaches the state of Cheerleading, they may stop buying. By catering to only best customers we ignore the potential all of the other customers represent. And, as in Eddie Bauer's case, we begin to believe that our best customers define us as a brand, when the truth of the matter is this audience aspires to the founding principle, believes in the founding principle, and aligns themselves with the core user. But they are not the core user.

The mistake to avoid is believing that your most avid buyer, your most profitable customer, defines your brand. They don't. They follow your brand because of what you stand for. They follow your core users because of what they stand for as well.

It's exactly this sort of thinking that has lead us historically to look at profitability as a byproduct of the performances of one-dimensional metrics, rather than looking at what truly contributes to profitability, which is long-term, sustainable buying behavior of not just our best customers, but all of our customers. It's the migration rates of all of our customers—the only way to accurately perceive that value is by considering every customer as an asset.

> "To manage customers as assets, you must be able to value them as assets. This means you must be able to quantify and predict customer duration and lifecycle cash flow."
>
> **FREDERICK REICHHELD AND THOMAS TEAL**
> *THE LOYALTY EFFECT*

It's astonishing how much data we collect these days trying to get a bead on our marketing efforts, drilling into our search, social media, catalogs, Web sites, and advertising efforts. The database junkies are busy spying on each individual customer's buying habits, tracking how much, how often, and how recently they've purchased. We're all busy measuring the performance of our tools, A/B testing, conversion rate optimization, etcetera. And a growing discipline under the heading of Big Data is the practice of predictive analytics. This is defined as mining deep pools of data to develop personalized recommendations on the products and services we all shop for and want next. It's predictive, meaning, if we know "X" about customer "Y" we should be able to anticipate the next most likely product Customer Y will want so we can push that recommendation to them and eke out another sale, another sale, another sale.

It is this relentless practice of marketing primarily to our best buyers that exemplifies our collective Linda Problem. According to Cabela's, they are the fishing and hunting category's "World's Foremost Outfitter." That may or may not be true. What *is* true is that they are experts at crunching Big Data, and they also have a very big Linda Problem.

Cabela's use of predictive analytics is a case in point:

> "So over the past couple of years, Cabela's has been relying heavily on predictive analytics software that draws on the mountain of data the company has generated from shoppers at its global Web site and its thirty stores across North America. Using tools from SAS Institute, a private company, Cabela's built a model that ranks customers from those with the best buying history to those with the worst. Next, it adds more than fifteen predictive variables, including a customer's preferred product categories and zip code. Each customer is then assigned a score from one to 100—the higher the 'star rating,' the greater the revenue projection. The score determines whether and when Cabela's mails that customer each of its catalogues.

> "The goal is 'to determine how much each customer is going to spend with us over the next twelve months,' says Corey Bergstrom, director of market research and analysis for the $2.6 billion company. Some high-value customers get special perks, such as more sophisticated telephone support. 'If you deserve the white-glove type treatment,' Bergstrom adds, 'we need to know who you are so that we can go the extra mile for you.'

"Since introducing the model, Cabela's has quadrupled the rate of responses to its catalogue. In other words, people who receive them are now four times as likely to buy something. It's reached a point, says Bergstrom, where 'we can predict what a customer is going to purchase next.' For instance, someone who purchased duck decoys might be in the market for a shotgun cleaning kit."

CINDY WAXER[xii]
MIT TECHNOLOGY REVIEW

The fascinating aspect of this "success" story is that Cabela's has deemed the program a success because of their focus on a one-dimensional metric: catalog response rate. This is a limited view of their consumer's real behavior. Quadrupling the response rate by sending catalogs to customers more likely to buy is not necessarily improving the performance of a catalog, it's just culling out unlikely buyers. Thinking that response rate is the key metric means they have to leave "nonperforming" customers off the mailing list. Seems a little unfair to say they improved the performance of their mailings when they are simply slicing off the bottom performers. What is happening to those customers? Where do they go? No white-glove treatment for them.

The interpretation that they can predict what a person is going to buy next is also erroneous. What they've really done is they've figured out who does not purchase and who does, and in some cases can see what products are likely purchased as bundles, even if they

---

xii   Cindy Waxer, "What Will Your Customers Buy Next?," *MIT Technology Review*, December 8, 2010. www.technologyreview.com/news/421928/what-will-your-customers-buy-next/

are purchased over time. In the end they've become very proficient delivering catalogs to only those customers with a high propensity to purchase, improving on the past based on their new analysis.

However, they can't see the forest for the trees. What about those customers that are not purchasing? Why aren't they buying? What's causing them to sit on the sidelines? What if there was a corresponding "white-glove-type treatment" for these customers?

Cabela's is succeeding wildly at one thing, while simultaneously making a much larger blunder by ignoring the Rate of Migration of their total buying population to becoming high value customers. Your best buying customers are a limited resource. Their buying power is finite.

Cabela's Model of Customer Management:

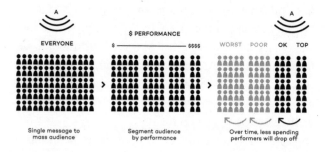

What remains largely ignored and massively misunderstood is Cabela's customers' path, or migration, to a future state of regular purchasing. Considering this conventional CRM approach over time, the implication is that eventually when a top performer's buying wanes, they are relegated to lesser and lesser status, and under performers are ignored entirely.

The diagram below defines the provider and user relationship in terms of valuing each segment based on where they are in their progression—a view of the Customer Activation model in direct comparison to the conventional model employed by Cabela's.

The Customer Activation Cycle Model

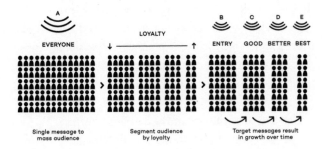

Your customers are *the* assets that contribute most tangibly to growth and profitability. It follows then that spending quality time and resources understanding their progression toward the end state of long-term, sustainable buying behavior will assure you're maximizing the potential from your most valuable assets: all of your customers.

Cabela's is focused on a transactional measure of a marketing vehicle, rather than using the power of their analytics to chart the overall progress of every customer. In essence, they are firing underperforming customers and pampering high-performing customers. This is the standard of the industry, and it's leaving vast numbers of customers behind rather than understanding clearly where the brand relationship is failing and pulling those customers along. This, in Kahneman's terms, is Cabela's Linda Problem. They've jumped to an intuitive conclusion about what their data is telling them: "If customer A buys lots of stuff, let's reward them; if customer B buys not so much, let's ignore them because it costs money to pamper them and they're not worth it." Cabela's marketers are missing that those underperforming customers represent potential future value. Although they are not frequent purchasers now, they very well could be at some point in the future.

Cabela's would be much more powerfully served if they were to measure the value of their customers, determine a monetary value of each segment (casuals, loyalists, and cheerleaders), then treat them like physical assets, recognizing the potential profit of migrating an under-performer to becoming a high-performer.

If we truly understand the dollar value of our best customers, the ones that buy from us year after year after year, the ones Cabela's is providing white-glove treatment to, we would then be compelled to ask this question: How good are we at turning low-value customers (the ones we stopped marketing to) into high-value customers (the ones that essentially contribute the lion's share of profit to our bottom line)?

Understanding the answer to this single question changes everything.

First, Kahneman and Tversky would be proud of us for looking more deeply at the evidence.

Second, observing migration rates ties the organizing principle to operations, marketing, and sales. It forces an organization to look at why customers are in certain categories and how best to move them around the cycle. The *why*, as we've seen, is a company's purpose—it's reason for being. Migration rate is the metric that ties contribution dollars to your core purpose via the qualitative Customer Activation Cycle.

And when it does, you can assure your customer is getting what they need to make the journey of discovery to become a high-contribution-dollar customer. Rather than abandoning low-performing customers, we endeavor to understand these customers' progression to becoming regular, repeat buyers. The goal is *more* cheerleaders, not *only* cheerleaders.

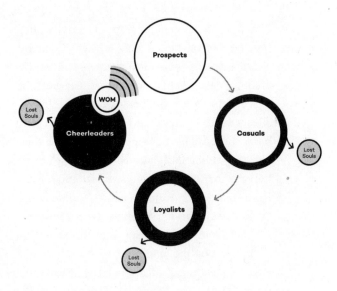

"A recent Gartner Inc. research study showed that 75% of managers planned to make further investments in CRM in the coming year.

However, most CRM systems have been used merely to categorize customers into segments based on their current levels of profitability. This approach may have implications for the bottom line, but it does little to advance the shift from mass marketing to one-to-one relationships. Customer *relationship* management has devolved into customer *profitability* management, a one-dimensional, company-centric practice based on economics and costs that provides little insight into why and in what ways people form relationships with companies and brands.

"That lack of relationship sensitivity has precipitated a new trend in which many companies use their CRM systems to identify and 'fire' low-revenue, high-cost customers. In a recent survey we conducted of 900 customers, 30% said that they knew someone who had been cut loose by a company with which they had a commercial relationship. We are not so naive as to think that companies should refrain from analyzing customers' purchase data or the efficiency of marketing dollars spent. However, we have found that basic information about customer lifetime value can be a limited and even misleading indicator of the status and potential of a customer relationship. Loyalty programs, the most basic type of CRM program, do surprisingly little to address relationship realities or build relationship bonds.

"Although CRM programs may prevent customers from taking their business elsewhere, they are less effective at identifying the reasons to encourage them to stay. Ironically, CRM programs themselves may actually contribute to the creation of high-cost, low-value customers. However you look at it, companies are doing something wrong."

SUSAN FOURNIER AND JILL AVERY[xiii]
MIT SLOAN MANAGEMENT REVIEW

If you measure how your customers are tracking toward loyalty, you're defining a much more nuanced and profound means of measuring success. One that determines if the path to loyalty has an offshoot that you didn't know about, like one that spins good, valuable customers off into a no man's land (lost souls, see diagram) soon to be swooped up by your competitors, or one that leads them to further and further depth of commitment to your brand, a more regular, repeatable buying pattern, and ultimately fandom.

xiii   Susan Fournier and Jill Avery, "Putting the 'Relationship' Back Into CRM," *MIT Sloan Management Review*, March 23, 2011. sloanreview.mit.edu/article/putting
-the-relationship-back-into-crm/

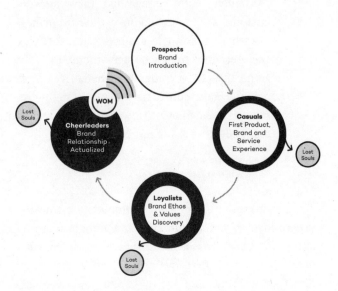

This is where theory and the qualitative nicety of brand identity, marketing messaging, and the definition of your "core" customer meets the harsh realities of the bottom line, measured in terms of migration of customer segments.

What amount of profit (minus marketing costs, COGS, and shipping costs) is your casual customer contributing? What amount of profit is your most loyal customer contributing? How long does it take to move your casual customers to become cheerleaders?

Add to this how much it costs you to acquire a casual customer, how many total casual, loyalist, and cheerleader customers you have, and the speed at which you can create that most valuable bucket of customers and you've got everything you need to determine the health and profitability of your entire enterprise. This then in total is the true value of your company.

The beauty of this approach is that identifying the respective answers to these questions provides a more accurate depiction of the holistic health of the organization than any one-dimensional measurement.

Here's how it looks:

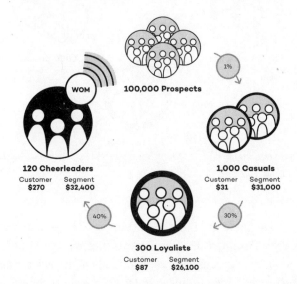

Efficiency of the progression is the key to success. The more efficiently customers migrate to become cheerleaders, the faster the value of the organization grows. The bottom line grows exponentially.

The magic bullet is to improve the Rate of Migration from one stage to the next by providing the correct customer experience at each milestone.

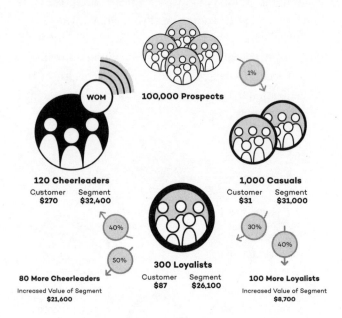

As noted in the MIT Sloan article, and in the Cabela's example, the standard practice is to continue to carve away at your database until only high-performing customers remain. This practice is entirely antithetical to building long-term, sustainable relationships. Rather, we need to diagnose what those first-time buyers are missing in experience, communication, or belief that is required to motivate them to the next stage and the next purchase.

Consider the Customer Activation Cycle in its full form—as a fractal:

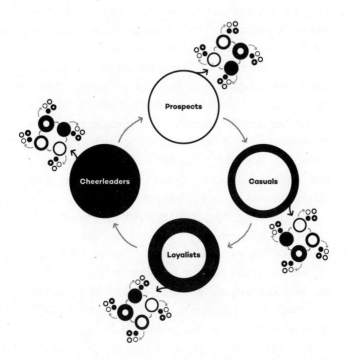

Customers move either to the next stage, or they attrit or deactivate. In old school direct marketing, like the Cabela's of the world, there is an attempt to "reactivate," and if the customer makes a purchase they are lumped right back into the bucket with "top performers." If they don't purchase again, these customers in the old school model simply become lost souls never to reengage with the brand again, or at least never to be communicated to again.

In the Customer Activation Cycle model, these "underperformers" are simply not activating to the next stage, they are moving back to a more nascent stage, which is fine. They are destined to remain prospects because they actually don't align with the first impression. If they do progress to the casual, loyalist, or cheerleader stages, that is not to say that at some point in their tenure they won't stop purchasing, or hesitate purchasing. If they were Cabela's customers, they'd be fired. In the Customer Activation Cycle viewed as a fractal, the "underperformers" simply reenter the cycle as prospects. And in that instance, they are respected as still highly qualified potential cheerleaders and begin their progression again. Hopefully, we discover why they've attrited and can remedy the cause.

The amazing thing about this visual representation is that it actually describes what truly happens in direct-marketing customer-performance databases over time. We see customers moving to different stages as they continue to progress, hesitate, progress, stop buying, reactivate, and on and on. In fact, unlike other models, this one accounts for customers that are "loyal" who don't actually buy over time. This model describes those customers as simply going dormant as a buyer, but they are still in the cycle as a prospect. This accounts for loyalists or cheerleaders that have a bad product experience, or get grumpy, but don't necessarily give up entirely being in love. They simply may not have the funds to continue a regular buying habit. Just because a customer stops purchasing doesn't mean they are not a fan. Because of their loyalty they stay in the fray defined as part of the likely world of prospects once again, holding the same needs and aligned beliefs as the brand, but simply having to retest their experience at different courses in their lifetime in relationship with the brand. The only remaining question we as marketers need to ask then is if a loyalist or cheerleader exits, what caused the exit and what then will bring them back into progressing through the cycle?

The brave new world is all about long-term sustainable relationships and avoiding the Linda Problem.

You've identified a target audience. You've crafted stories to communicate your appeal to that audience. You've built a marketing plan and budgeted dollars dedicated to distributing those messages to that target audience. And now you're set to measure the performance of the market, your message, and your distribution. The old formula was simply, "Will enough people respond and buy enough stuff, at a high enough price such that at the end of the day you have a profit remaining?" If that formula works, you're in business.

That's no longer how to compete. There is so much competition in every space that for every Apple there are thousands of Dells, for every Patagonia there are thousands of Cloudveils. There remain only a few winners that capture the headlines, but there are thousands more losers that simply can't sustain regular buying habits from their customers.

To compete, your brand must win the hearts and minds of your target audience and your brand must continue to win the hearts and minds of your existing customers. If your brand can't connect meaningfully enough and uniquely engage prospects, casuals, and loyalists such that they are migrating to the next segment, ultimately your brand will not create enough cheerleaders fast enough to viably sustain your organization. Period. Knowing that cheerleaders are typically worth ten to twelve times as much as casual customers in terms of contribution, without cheerleaders there are simply not enough contribution dollars to maintain profitability.

If, in fact, you choose to further and further slice away "underperforming" customers, you'll be forced to continue to squeeze pennies from a more and more isolated segment of customers, the "high performers" only. This is the lesson learned at Patagonia in the late nineties when the lightbulb went off for us.

Our direct marketing strategy was all about this same one-dimensional approach, measuring only the catalog response rate. The problem was, again, a frog in a frying pan. While focusing only on this metric over time, we neglected to highlight that the total number of loyal customers was not growing year to year. A strategy of mailing deep into our "loyal" house file as a means to buoy financial returns for several years had left our acquisition of new-to-file customers depleted and our loyal customers spending habits exhausted. Slowly but surely our catalog response rate waned. Only when we began looking at the migration rates of customers did we realize there was a smarter way to manage our business, and a means that aligned with our corporate values. We came to understand that, in order for Patagonia customers to become fanatical buyers, they had to progress through the stages of falling in love. Firing them early in their progression was counterintuitive once we gleaned this understanding.

The mental framework defined by the Customer Activation Cycle governed the strategy at Patagonia beginning in 2006. It sparked the turn around of the direct business that continues to grow at double-digit pace today. For a privately held organization with a slow growth mentality, the shift was stunning.

This same thinking also explains why Apple currently holds the most cash reserves of any company on the market today, upward of $164.4 billion. Besides not paying dividends, it's because they've practiced this equation to a T. Blink to test to bond to love—their cash comes from the process of creating cheerleaders. Customers all along the cycle of the Customer Activation Cycle getting what they need when they need it lead to increased buying and progression to fanaticism.

Understanding this logic and how to then manage the migration of your prospects to become cheerleaders should be the focal point of everything you do.

Seth Godin's "Four questions worth answering"[xiv]:

1. Who is your next customer? (Conceptually, not specifically. Describe his outlook, his tribe, his hopes and dreams and needs and wants...)

2. What is the story he told himself (about the world, about his situation, about his perceptions) before he met you?

3. How do you encounter him in a way that he trusts the story you tell him about what you have to offer?

4. What change are you trying to make in him, his life, or his story?

---

xiv   Seth Godin, "Four questions worth answering," November 26, 2012. sethgodin.typepad.com/seths_blog/2012/11/four-questions-worth-answering.html

Start with this before you spend time on tactics, technology, or scalability.

With the Customer Activation Cycle model in hand, this advice becomes a pragmatic and valuable tool by applying the understanding gleaned about your customer and making actionable steps that are measureable. These are the fundamentals of creating a step-by-step progression that will create true, long-term, sustainable, loyal customer relationships. This is true CRM. Anything less is merely customer "contact" management, not Customer Relationship Management.

Building on Godin's commentary, we can layer this qualitative ideal of customer understanding with quantitative understanding of how well you are developing trust with the consumer at each stage of the relationship as they move from blink to test to bond to love.

The simple rule is to communicate and develop the appropriate customer experience for each segment of customer in the Customer Activation Cycle based on their particular needs.

People are interested in their own needs and their own opinions. Everyone is different. Customers behave that way as well, which is why customers new to a brand have different expectations, product and service needs, and information requirements than long-term, loyal customers.

It's imperative your brand's story is clear and well-executed with content, community, and commerce based on general brand values and beliefs. However, avoid the pitfall of communicating en masse with your constituency. Instead, consider the granular aspects of your customers' experience based on their tenure with you. Your promotional campaigns, navigation paths, and merchandising schemes can speak to new customers specific to their needs and loyal customers specific to theirs.

Taking it Personally

My family says I take everything too personally. I guess that's why I'm so easily offended by how companies treat me. I've been buying dishwashing liquid from Seventh Generation for twenty years, along with Method, Ecover, and Begley's Best. None of them know it or seem to care. Do they offer replenishment services on their sites? Do they send me emails telling me how I can make my home free of other toxins? Any recommendations on cool new products I might like as a service? Perhaps they've recommended a green dry cleaner or home cleaning service in my neighborhood? Nope, nope, nope, and nope. Maybe if one of them had, somewhere along the line made an effort to include me in their cause, their purpose, the inkling of their true character, I would be loyal to that one brand. But I'm not. I buy across the spectrum...just look under my sink.

I recently reread an old *Fast Company* article by Bill Breen that noted a trend called *luxe populi*, which is the quest to stay visible in an increasingly invisible world by becoming one of the "important people." Luxe populi is a deeply held, even militant belief that we are all entitled to the very finest, the best designed, and the coolest things. Intriguing. Maybe this is at the root of my issue with how brands treat me, which is to say, as not special.

Here's the big question: Why do loyal, multi-purchase, long-term customers get the same offering of product and content as first time customers, or even worse, prospective customers? Cabela's is at least making an effort to treat long-time buyers differently, albeit, by sending catalogs, discounts, and other perks. But I'm talking about meaningful content related to purpose.

In this day of instantaneous communication, news, content, and service, it's simple to aggregate customers into different segments based on their needs and desires and then build content campaigns, Web sites, email communications, and video and marketing campaigns that connect at a deeper level with these customers, the people brand managers hope to serve. More and more products and brands are being commoditized. The brands that listen and connect with their customers create at least a foundation of understanding for loyalty. Those that don't have to circle back and spend more money a second or third time, continuing to compete over and over again for the same customer...it's a zero-sum game.

Old school, mass marketers need to give up the idea that one cool brand message is the panacea. It's not. Consumers want their particular needs met. They want to be heard, they want a voice, and brands that give them a voice will win their business. Giving customers a voice means brands have to listen, and they have to respond to what they hear. When they do, the money will follow.

A Case of Improved Migration...prAna Living

Anchored in the outdoor industry, prAna was an early player in yoga and climbing. In the midst of the 2008 recession, however, prAna, an eighteen-year-old brand at the time, had lost market share in the ever-exploding category of yoga, primarily lead by

Lululemon's expansion into retail. In addition to getting out-maneuvered by Lululemon, prAna found itself up against a ceiling in both the world of climbing and distribution opportunities in the outdoor marketplace. And so my work with them began.

We painstakenly invested in a process of self-evaluation, which included reaching out to customers, conducting in-depth interviews, listening intently and objectively, and finally constructing a Customer Activation Cycle. The founder and executive team had suspicions about tapping their roots of mindfulness. Was the market ready for a progressive perspective? Were they alone in their belief in mindfulness practices? The process of discovery revealed in the construct of the Customer Activation Cycle that there was more than simply a like-minded audience that was connecting with prAna, but actually a desire among prAna core buyers for them to be more vocal and forthcoming about their key brand ethos. This revelation buoyed confidence and so began the process of devising an omni-channel strategy dedicated to bringing the qualities of the prAna belief system to the surface at every possible touch point.

> "Breath, life, vitality of the spirit. These qualities infuse not only our name, but also our aspirations, the things we make and how we make them. Welcome to mindfully designed, built to last products—born from the experience."

The refreshing of an eighteen-year-old brand provides an opportunity to also look deep into the quantitative side of the equation—the math. Migration is the key indicator of the health and wellness of long-term, sustainable customer relationships. In late 2009, prAna's challenge was early migration. Attraction to the brand was a matter of capturing interest via a compelling product presentation and style, but migrating consumers beyond the early stage of infatuation required an overall improved product experience, and getting consumers all the way around the cycle to an actualized brand relationship would require clear, real-world examples of the depth and breadth of the brand values of mindfulness.

The resulting strategy lead to the implementation of a new Web site, the launch of a direct to consumer catalog, the development of a relational marketing database, and a fully integrated social media and customer acquisition strategy in concert with a new, branded look and feel. From 2011 through 2013, prAna was the fastest growing company in the outdoor industry.

The organizing principle behind all of these plans was a fully enacted Customer Activation Cycle. Each segment of customer type was described in detail with accompanying merchandising presentations and strategic communications. Those anemic migration rates of casuals and loyalists turned to robust migration rates. Rather than firing those underperformers, each segment was assigned a value in terms of contribution dollars, and with that assignment, recognition that every customer counted.

The reality is that direct marketing strategy works well to define who, what, when, and where. But it misses "Why?" Why do customers buy from one brand versus another? Why do they become advocates? Why do they choose to register for a brand credit card, or choose to register on a Web site? Why do they vote with their dollars to support brands that are cause oriented?

At the heart of the reasoning behind the why are more than demographics, personas, and statistical likelihoods; there are qualities the consumer experiences while engaging with that brand. The subtle triggers they react to emotionally in a positive way. The beauty of the Customer Activation Cycle is as an operational model, as a means to enact your merchandising and communications strategy. It is the tool that defines exactly how these qualitative aspects of brand affinity contribute to the bottom line.

You can now identify the progression of a prospect along the path to becoming a loyal, long-term buyer, a cheerleader. You can enact a tracking and measurement system that accurately predicts the following: How long it takes to create that cheerleader, how much they will spend along the way, how many cheerleaders you can create over a given period of time, and how much that group as a collective whole will contribute in profit at some point in the future. Moreover, you are not leaving valuable "underperforming" customers behind, just identifying where your communications and actions have underperformed. You are providing customers with what they need to become your best cheerleaders.

"To be confused about what
is different is to be confused
about everything."

DAVID BOHM

CHAPTER SEVEN

Errors in Judgment

A new lens on performance sheds light on the flaws of commonly held beliefs. Knowing that customers are ultimately attached to why things are the way they are more so than what they are compels one to view the world of communication differently. Following are examples of how many common practices previously accepted as best practices lose their luster when viewed in terms of customer migration.

Error #1: Being Customer Centric

According to Forrester Research: "It's the age of the customer...[which puts] the customer at the center of your strategy." If an auto maker put the customer at the center of their strategy, they'd likely be making a Ferrari and selling it for zero down, zero at closing, and zero per month, forever. Putting the customer at the center of your strategy is a precarious notion. Just ask the managers of Eddie Bauer. Instead, devise a strategy that reflects your core purpose, beliefs, and values and put that at the center of your business. Then integrate this in its entirety into every aspect of your value chain, communicating your purpose clearly to your customers as they migrate to become cheerleaders. Patagonia succeeds over time because of a strict adherence to principles. This is clear in Patagonia's Reason for Being:

"Our values reflect those of a business started by a band of climbers and surfers, and the minimalist style they promoted. The approach we take toward product design demonstrates a bias for simplicity and utility.

"For us at Patagonia, a love of wild and beautiful places demands participation in the fight to save them, and to help reverse the steep decline in the overall environmental health of our planet. We donate our time, services and at least 1% of our sales to hundreds of grassroots environmental groups all over the world who work to help reverse the tide.

"We know that our business activity—from lighting stores to dyeing shirts—creates pollution as a by-product. So we work steadily to reduce those harms. We use recycled polyester in many of our clothes and only organic, rather than pesticide-intensive, cotton."

Patagonia's values drive their behavior and decision-making. They not only connect with their customers that way, they help influence them as well.

Error #2: Focusing on Increasing Sales Within the Customer Segments with the Greatest Lifetime Value

All customers start their brand relationships with only a cursory understanding. They then move to a point of trust, and eventually to deeper and deeper understanding of values and shared beliefs. With affirming experiences along the way and aligned beliefs, they become committed, long lasting, loving fans following the path from blink to test to bond to love. By focusing on migration of customers from their point of entry you'll realize in the end a greater number of customers with high lifetime value. This is imperative. Abandoning low performing customers is the equivalent of finding fault with the user. Explore that relationship further and discover what in the brand/service environment is not resonating, and then shore up the communication or the user experience that will communicate more effectively the idealized state of the relationship.

Error #3: Focusing on First Impressions

You only get to make a good impression once. You also only get to make that first impression one time. Mass marketing communicates one thing, the broad stroke, over and over again. This is fine as an introduction, but long-term customers grow tired of hearing the same story. Show respect for these folks. Treat them like they are part of the exclusive club they truly are, which doesn't mean a series of rewards and perks, nor does it mean hitting them over the head with the same brand mantra day in and day out. Give them something more.

A better strategy is to engage with them to be part of something that is meaningful relative to the shared value set. Connect them to transcendent purpose, make them part of your tribe. Go beyond blink.

Error #4: Not Sticking to Your Principles

A big MINI? Sometimes a product hits the market and fires on all cylinders. No pun intended, but that was the case in 2002 when BMW rereleased the iconic

MINI Cooper. Originally designed by Alec Isigonis and launched into the British market in 1959, the MINI Cooper was nimble and quick, a driving experience unparalleled. Tiny, with a low center of gravity, and a relatively wide footprint, and yet a four-passenger, functionally valid car, and super fun. The Brit's answer to the Porsche's VW Beetle back in the day, which Porsche countered with the 911 in 1965, but that's another story.

Forty-three years later, BMW reintroduced the world to the simple thrill of driving. Rather than top-end speed and performance statistics, it was all about the feel of being a little kid driving a go-kart—pure fun. "Let's Motor" was for people who loved the idea of the original coupe— its maneuverability and playful cornering—all while accommodating four passengers. This wasn't grand touring, this was rally car driving, reinvigorated with modern technology, that was the idea when BMW reintroduced the classic MINI Cooper as simply "The MINI."

The accompanying marketing campaign was all about being part of a tribe of driving enthusiasts.

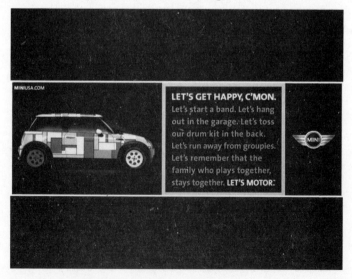

Fast forward to 2012. It's all gone awry. What happened? The 2012 model is playing to a new theme.

> "With its heavily raked windshield and chopped greenhouse, the MINI Coupe presents a tougher and more sport-oriented image than the already zippy standard car...focused on optimum performance."
>
> **NICK KURCZEWSKI**[xv]
> *ROAD & TRACK*

High performance is BMW's credo; however, the MINI is a MINI, not a BMW. The MINI isn't "The Ultimate Driving Machine." The MINI was the ultimate avant-garde driving statement. The 2012 models proved a far cry from the essence of what a true MINI has been for fifty-three years: *fun*.

Not to dive into the weeds, but the four-seater's wheelbase is longer, it's taller, the cargo capacity is greater. A big MINI? *Blasphemous!*

This is the antithesis of great product development and branding, and even worse nurturing of loyalty— the equivalent of the frog in the frying pan. Straying from the core reason for being portends a slow death of whatever brand the iconic product represents. It happened to Eddie Bauer in the eighties and nineties as they shifted from being "expedition outfitters" to "active casual outfitters."

When brands begin to cater to their largest contingent of buyers, they've forgotten that those buyers are followers. The mistake is forgetting why the brand was founded in the first place, why the large population of fringe customers becomes the largest

xv   Nick Kurczewski, "Caught Testing: 2012 MINI Coupe—Spy Shots," *Road & Track*, February 9, 2011. www.roadandtrack.com/new-cars/future-cars/news/a16919
/caught-testing-2012-mini-coupe/

contingent of buyers. That large audience is made up of late adopters, or followers. The followers are the people living the dream vicariously by following the leaders. These are not the core that led the charge at the outset.

Authentic brands are born from inspiration, from a spark of a new perspective. This spark is what the first buyers connect with and are inspired to take a chance on and buy. As those buyers adopt the new, others follow, growth ensues, and sometimes a tipping point is reached and the masses follow.

Sadly, BMW is chasing the masses by producing a car that "has broader appeal": more aggressive, more powerful, the four-seater is nearly twice the size of Alec Isigonis' original inspiration.

Founded in 1959, rebirthed in 2002, sentenced to death in 2012.

Error #5: Not Having Principles

The perfect example is the Nook. Barnes & Noble was founded in 1873 and grew through the years by providing a vast offering of books made convenient via retail brick-and-mortar stores. They are neighborhood booksellers through and through. However, with the onset of the Internet, e-commerce, and digital technologies, rather than being true to their principles as neighborhood booksellers, they decided to look at technology as a core competence. This mistake is exemplified in the Nook.

As of 2013, B&N was still the largest independent bookseller and does sell a lot of Nooks, but they still haven't made a profit with their e-reader, even though they've dedicated a significant presence in their stores and have a captured audience to market the product to. Analysts ask, "Why?" The answer is simple: it's not why

B&N exists. The Nook is an outlier product that is not part of the B&N's reason for being. It does not support "neighborhood bookseller."

Amazon leads the category with the Kindle, and Apple ultimately has become the real winner on the e-reader battlefield because they provide something beyond just the tool. Apple customers are loyal to the brand and buy the array of Apple products because there is something there that they believe in. It's not about the product. It's about how that product fits the overall equation.

> "Revenue from the company's Nook division for its fiscal 2013 third quarter declined 26% from the same period a year ago, primarily as a result of slumping sales of the devices. Is the bookseller just losing ground to rival Amazon and its market-leading line of Kindles? Perhaps. But many tech analysts see something else happening: the booming market for tablet computers is starting to make the dedicated e-reader obsolete. 'It's not that the Nook failed,' said James McQuivey, a digital analyst at Forrester Research. 'It's that the world of tablets exploded, going faster than anyone expected, putting us in a place where tablets are now a fundamental part of our computing and lifestyle entourage, not just a handy device to consume a bit of media.' Apple rocked the computing world in 2010 with the release of the iPad, introducing the world to the concept of user-friendly tablets. While they already existed in some form, tablets were pretty much unknown to all but the most tech-savvy among

us. Since then, all Apple has done is sell more than 120 million of them."

DOUG GROSS[xvi]
CNN

Apple wins because they are selling the belief that "thinking different can change the universe." If you believe in that, you buy Apple. Changing the universe is Apple's job. They do it through technology. Their technology will always be evolving. B&N is a bookseller. Why would customers get behind their technology? Simply put, there's not an underlying principle driving this product line for B&N. Their principles are about being booksellers, not technology competitors. A big, costly mistake easily avoided with a simple focus on core principles.

Error #6: Having the Wrong Principles

Groupon started out life in 2007 as The Point, a social media platform designed to crowdsource campaigns for social good. The Point was cause-oriented; it leveraged technology and social media to enable groups of people to come together to solve problems. It worked by enabling individuals to form groups that would not normally know one another or have the opportunity to cross paths and assemble. The Point was a pretty cool idea. It was never really conceived to make money. The founder, Andrew Mason, like many entrepreneurs, wanted to change the world for the better.

Then one day some of The Point's users collectively recognized that The Point could be used to bring individuals together to make group purchases that

xvi   Doug Gross, "As Tablets Boom, E-readers Feel the Blast," CNN, February 28, 2013. www.cnn.com/2013/02/28/tech/gaming-gadgets/tablets-replacing-e-readers/

would constitute discounts; discounts to all sorts of activities, and for all sorts of goods. Normally, folks used The Point to organize around a cause for doing "good." This group decided their cause was saving money.

Coincidently, right around this time the global economy began to tumble in September 2008, the founders, Andrew Mason and Eric Lefkosky, decided it was time to take the group buying idea and pursue it in earnest. Groupon was born from the necessity of circumstances: the coincidence of a good idea and a bad economy. As quickly as this new opportunity emerged, The Point faded to the background and became a footnote to the fastest growing company in history.

Groupon became a deal-making machine. By the end of the first quarter of 2011 Groupon had 83 million subscribers, $645 million in sales and a $30 billion valuation, all built on a simple premise: exposure and customer acquisition for the vendor and a great price for the consumer. Strategically, Groupon distinguished itself with an unparalleled data mining backend and a humorous personality on the front end. Their approach was to "be the first and be the biggest." This worked until the competition recognized there was little barrier to entry. Soon, a myriad of copycats jumped in the game, companies you may or may not have heard of such as Swoop, HomeRun, Scoop, and Adility. Soon, however, bigger players like Living Social started to encroach on Groupon's dominance. In August of 2011, Amazon entered the fray, prompting Andrew Mason to make this statement:

> "Not only must we beat the thousands of clones who lifted our idea and began at roughly the same time as we did, but now we must also beat the biggest, smartest technology companies in the world. They are coming HARD.

> "By this time next year, we will either be on our way to becoming one of the great technology brands that define our generation, or a cool idea by people who were out-executed and out-innovated by others that were smarter and harder working."

In early 2012, given the circumstances that surrounded Groupon, they had a choice. To continue to chase more proprietary technology-based services that might make Groupon hard to replicate, or to reimagine their founding inspiration and establish a firm footing regarding their strategic purpose. Quite possibly, they could evolve their service offering from this perspective.

The writing was on the wall. Groupon clearly chose to out-duel the competition with superior technology. Being a promotionally oriented commodity marketer is all about the best deal. If there is no other purpose associated with serving that deal, then eventually someone is going to do it better. By the summer of 2013, Groupon had lost approximately half its value since its initial public offering in November 2011.

> "Our primary vision is to build out a marketplace which people can come to when they have a need... We're fortunate that Groupon is inherently mobile by nature. We're very focused on that. We're also focused on this fundamental shift in consumer behavior."
>
> **ERIC LEFKOSKY**[xvii]
> *BLOOMBERG NEWS*

---

xvii   Douglas MacMillan, "Groupon Pins Turnaround on Billionaire Investor Lefkofsky," *Bloomberg News*, August 8, 2013. www.bloomberg.com/news/articles/2013-08-08/groupon -pins-turnaround-on-billionaire-investor-lefkofsky

Chasing the customer with deals and discounts proved to not be a defensible position. The first mover advantage has faded. Technology is still not Groupon's strength, at least not relative to Amazon. So, where does Groupon turn?

In 2008 the founders rationalized the shift from being cause-oriented to being deal-oriented.

> "[The] way we rationalized it with ourselves, [was that we were] helping people find interesting things to do in their city."[xviii]

It would be interesting to rewind the clock and see what Groupon would have become had they still pursued group buying as a service, but in the context of a company truly focused on the greater good.

Error #7: Going Broke Saving Money

Well, actually, the phrase should be "going broke giving money away," but it's not as funny. I'm a pretty normal customer. I fly here and there with some frequency, rent cars, do some of the grocery shopping for the household, and buy my clothing with my wife's advice. I also am chased by loyalty programs of every shape and size. There's lots of science regarding how well those programs motivate folks. It's surprising they mostly still exist, because, for the most part, the science doesn't support the claims.

One great example is a little restaurant chain here in Southern California called Native Foods. They have

xviii   Nicholas Carlson, "Inside Groupon: The Truth About The World's Most
Controversial Company," *Business Insider*, October 31, 2011. www.businessinsider.com
/inside-groupon-the-truth-about-the-worlds-most-controversial-company-2011-10

a couple locations I frequent as I drive through LA and Orange County, but none near my home, so I make a point of stopping whenever I'm in their neighborhood. The reason I stop by is because of my loyalty card. Just kidding. I'm a vegetarian and the restaurant is vegan and the chef/founder puts together some of the tastiest dishes I've ever had, vegetarian or otherwise. Even though this is California, finding vegan restaurants is not that easy. Especially those that are reasonably priced, have a variety of interesting dishes, and are quick and easy to access. I eat at Native Foods for all of these reasons. It's a treat for me.

I do have a loyalty card that the guy at the counter *made* me get, and every tenth time I visit I get a little discount amounting to the near equivalent of a free meal. That's nice, but I really don't need it. I'd stop and eat regardless of the loyalty card. Price isn't terribly significant in this case because I'm desperate to find good vegetarian fare when I'm on the road. I'm wondering if the management really understands what that card is doing for them. Is it motivating folks to choose Native Foods versus the Black Angus down the street?

Loyalty is all about the experience, connecting with the core values of your constituents. If you're competing within the confines of the harsh world of commodities, then maybe the discounts provided by loyalty programs make a difference. Being promotional is a valid strategy in that instance. But, if you've distinguished your company with your offer, product, positioning, or service, your customers are going to respond with their loyal behavior. One of the greatest benefits of having loyal customers is the fact they pay premium pricing. Generally speaking, within non-commodity categories, half of all customers will pay a 20% to 25% premium for their favorite brand before switching to another. That's a lot of money.

Rather than giving rewards to your loyal customers, deliver on your brand promise at every point of interaction and take those dollars you may be giving away and apply them to your bottom line, or a worthy cause, or an employee benefit program, and save us fans the hassle of another card in our wallet.

Error #8: Thinking That Customers in the 21st Century are Fundamentally Different Than Customers in the 20th Century

The evolution of the human species is slow and meandering. In the past one hundred years, there are truly only imperceptible differences in people, and they're mostly physical. We still fight wars. We still fall in love. We are nationalistic. And, we are brand aware.

Our environment has changed, and the gadgets we distract ourselves with are ever-changing. The stuff we buy is cooler, faster, stronger. But the fundamental motivation of why people choose one vendor versus another is steeped in beliefs and needs. It's been that way from the beginning of the mercantile trade, and regardless of the next digital phenom, eco-friendly automobile, fashion-forward clothing company, or technical wizardry that comes to market, if it meets our needs or supports our beliefs, we'll forge a relationship.

Error #9: Using Personas

That Ferrari mentioned a bit ago is priced at the top of the market. Is it just wealth that defines a Ferrari customer or is there more? Are Ferrari buyers adventurous? Do they love design? Red? Are they fans of auto racing? History? Are they exclusively male? Are they older or younger? All good questions. The answers, however, ultimately don't matter. A modern marketer would likely be compelled to pen a persona, a characterization of the ideal target customer in order to configure the perfect positioning of the Ferrari brand. Not Enzo Ferrari. He built the legend focusing on his passion.

Enzo Ferrari was born in 1898, began driving racing cars in 1919 when he was twenty-one, and officially launched his own company branded Ferrari in 1947 with the street-legal 125 S, powered by a 1.5 L V12 engine. This was the first V12 ever made available to consumers. He designed and manufactured cars in such a way that the cars themselves "perfectly represented the concepts of winning, technology, performance, and style." His focus was always on racing, but it was the car that stirred him. So much so that as a driver he was famously known to care so much for the cars he drove that he would never bring himself to risk ruining them to win the race. In fact, the production company that bore his name existed entirely to fund his racing program. To further demonstrate his strict adherence to his principles, the Dino released in 1968, among the street legal production series, was not even released under the Ferrari name because it didn't sport a twelve-cylinder engine and simply was too domesticated in Enzo's opinion to be a Ferrari.

> "There was something innovative about Ferraris that other cars did not have, and the man who created them was extraordinary: pleasant, curious, biting, overpowering, and conciliatory.

He exploited every opportunity with a mixture of managerial skills and missionary zeal..."

PAOLO MARZOTTO
FERRARI 1947-1997

Enzo Ferrari was known as much for his design innovations as he was for his marketing, which was essentially an extension of his passion and his principles. The crest, the yellow background, the signature red, all had their origins in Enzo's home country, his family, and in racing. Ferrari has embodied Enzo's beliefs for more than six decades. As a result the product has stayed true to its core from the beginning.

Stop penning personas and start penning your values. Share your beliefs. Demonstrate how they integrate into your product, design, and presentation. Communicate what inspires your particular aesthetic. Those that believe what you believe will become part of your tribe.

10) Thinking Brand Equity is All in the Name, a Tagline, or a Campaign.

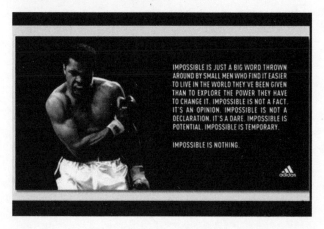

Quick, what does Adidas do that makes them a company worth buying from? Is "Impossible is Nothing" a shared value of yours? Do you believe Adidas believes in achieving the impossible? And, if so, how? Where does the rubber meet the road? The tagline is intriguing no doubt, and Ali as an iconic figure. That he overcame adversity multiple times throughout his life experience is inspiring. But is there more evidence that Adidas is about overcoming obstacles? If so, it would be very cool to understand how. Have they overcome some barrier in their production process that improves the lives of their workers? Is there something they've contributed to that allowed individuals to overcome a life limitation? Did their management at some point in their history overcome all odds to become the company they are today?

I don't know, do you? If there were those background stories somehow linked to this imagery, maybe I'd buy a lot more Adidas, because maybe I'd remember to buckle down and fight a bit harder in the midst of my next personal challenge because I'd be reminded of the shining example of someone else who did with a simple glance at my shoes.

Patagonia, on the other hand, has no tagline, just a mission. They demonstrate their mission by challenging us to participate in what they believe in. Patagonia's critics call them sanctimonious. The reality is that there is substance behind what they do. It's not perfect, but the intention is true and is manifest in as many aspects of the organization, product, and service as possible within the constraints of operating a profitable business.

There are those who do what they believe in spite of criticism. This is why Patagonia has some of the most loyal followers on the planet, because those followers clearly get who Patagonia is and why they are in business, and they even get to participate in the cause. Some in small ways and some through actual activism, but regardless, if you wear the label you're reminded of the cause and that in some small way you're making a contribution by supporting what you believe is the right way to do things.

Conclusion: The Lazy Language of Loyalty

What's the first thing that pops into your head when you think of the word loyalty?

Points? Airlines? Free? For me, it's Toyota and my dog.

The term "loyalty" and its associated meaning has been dumbed down to effectively mean giving your customers something, or paying them in some way, to stick around and keep buying from you. It's disconcerting. Rarely is the word loyalty used to refer to a relationship, and more rarely is the word loyalty used to describe advocates.

Ideally, loyalty should conjure up a vision of your organization's actions: the actions that lead to committed behavior from your customers. Do you know what that actions are? Do you know where the missteps are? Do you know how healthy your relationship (loyalty) truly is?

Next time you think about loyalty, boil it down to the little things: how well your business is performing at the tiny nuances that mean the most to your customers. Loyalty resides between the cracks, in the miniscule moments that occur between a sales person and a customer, in the package they unwrap, or in the button they can or can't find to click online.

Think of the word loyalty in these terms, and the path to achieving it will be much more clear.

The world appears to be moved by Super Bowl ads, loyalty programs, and snappy taglines; but upon further examination, the reality is that these efforts are vastly less effective than the advertising agencies promoting them would care to admit. The classic example is the efficacy of the celebrated "Got Milk?" campaign. Common opinion is that this was one of the greatest advertising success stories in history. The truth of the matter is that even though the campaign boasts a 98% recall rate, between 1995 (when the campaign went national) and 2011 the yearly consumption of milk declined in the US from nearly twenty-four gallons per person to roughly twenty gallons per person, an eight percent decrease. Even in its initial year in California, where the campaign was first launched and focused, sales of milk rose only a paltry two percent.

More often than not, the time and money spent on ad campaigns, jingles, and promotions is done without understanding the deeper motivations of the potential buyer, causing mediocre results. Does a big MINI appeal to a driving enthusiast? Or is this a case of chasing the dog walker? Do airline miles really cause loyalty? Or did Southwest prove convenience trumps mileage? Does "Just Do It" get people off the couch? Or does Nike succeed by simply outspending the competition? And, did milk consumption decrease because people forgot how well it goes with Oreos? Apparently not. Something else was afoot. Awards aside, strategic planning has to start with an understanding of human behavior. Before anything, when devising strategy, first answer the question: "Why do we buy?"

> "Critical thinking demands that strategists consider a range of potential root causes for any given problem, and then develop a range of solutions before identifying the optimal one. Consumer research is a vital part of the process. When I see failure, it is often because root causes were never identified."
>
> **GENE DEL VECCHIO**[xix]
> ADJUNCT PROFESSOR OF MARKETING,
> USC MARSHALL SCHOOL OF BUSINESS

The following chapter presents how loyalty happens and examines how companies can leverage macro consumer behavior to more effectively engender long-term sustainable customer relationships.

---

xix   Gene Del Vecchio, "Got Milk? Got Fired: 5 Valuable Lessons That All Executives
Must Heed," *HuffPost Business*, April 6, 2015. www.huffingtonpost.com/gene-del-vecchio
/got-milk-got-fired-5-valu_b_4938176.html

"Man's general way of thinking of the totality, i.e. his general world view, is crucial for overall order of the human mind itself.

"If he thinks of the totality as constituted of independent fragments, then that is how his mind will tend to operate, but if he can include everything coherently and harmoniously in an overall whole that is undivided, unbroken and without border (for every border is a division or break) then his mind will tend to move in a similar way, and from this will flow an orderly action within the whole."

DAVID BOHM

CHAPTER EIGHT

The Macro View

Thus far the discussion has focused on the granular interactions and the cognitive processes of users and providers—this is the micro view of how brands attract a constituency. Explaining how the corner store succeeds or how Coke and Pepsi forge their daily battle requires a broader view of the competitive playing fields.

In chemistry, a bond describes the unique combining power of an element. In brand relationships, a bond is the unique strength of the connection that creates and sustains long-term relationships. Different types of business models and marketing approaches have different intensities of bonds. Some are weak, and some are strong. The force is very much like gravitational pull, the stronger the pull the closer the orbit. The weaker the bond the easier it is for a customer to simply fall out of orbit, drift away, and be pulled into a competing orbit. The good news is, the circumstances that dictate that gravitational pull, or force, enacted on the consumer are strategic choices brand managers can make proactively.

The strength of any Loyalty Bond ultimately depends on the type of business, brand positioning, merchandising scheme, and values at play within the organization. Assuring a strong brand bond is a matter of understanding and strategically managing these forces.

Brands, service providers, political parties, educational institutions, and organizations of all shapes and sizes exist because they provide some sort of end perceived benefit to the user. It's rather simple. We need stuff to live our lives. Some of it is frivolous and some of it is necessary for life. Regardless of where the particular service or product lands on the spectrum, consumers form their bond with the provider based on five simple precepts each with a unique disposition:

The Five Bonds of Loyalty

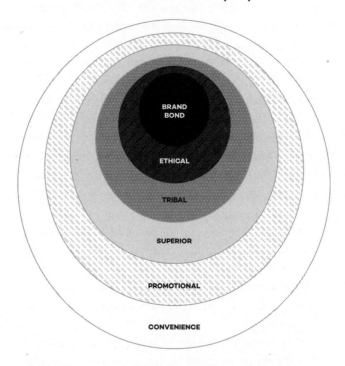

Collaboration with David Holifield, founder and owner of INTERFuel, an interactive design agency.

What follows is a look at each of the Five Bonds of Loyalty as seen in exemplary brands. I show caveats, provide clarity where there is often confusion, and recognize winners and losers as a means to identify the prime takeaway, or lesson learned, for each brand.

Convenience

Convenience is what the British call a Public Toilet. In America, we call it handy. And, believe it or not, this is the simplest and most straightforward way to win loyalty. Put the product, service, or brand at the consumer's fingertips. Allow the consumer to access your goods and make a choice with as little effort as possible. Make it easy. Call it convenient. Call it the corner store. Call it the Public Toilet.

The shining example of leveraging loyalty by convenience is Amazon. What started as an easier way to buy a book has become the easiest way to buy anything, especially if you as a customer have a premium (Prime) account and enjoy the luxury of free shipping. There is arguably no easier way to purchase goods online than Amazon, and they have the loyalty and frequency of purchasing to prove their model works. Amazon boasts 215 million active customers as of 2013, which at the time was nearly 70% of the US population.

Caveat

It's certainly possible to be the only one in your category to win on convenience; however, this strategy as a means to attain and assure loyalty is easily encroached on by competitors. Blockbuster painfully learned this lesson as they built their empire on convenience and seemingly had won the day. Then Netflix stole their thunder. Now Blockbuster has been forced to counter with an equally convenient service. The strategy is clear. Who achieves the most convenient model remains to be seen. In the meantime, it's great to be a consumer as the battle rages on. Watching movies gets easier and easier for us consumers.

An Example of Optimization by Zappos

Zappos' excellent business model and resulting loyalty is often seen as the result of stellar customer service. In fact, their growth followed the moment the founders and executive management finally settled on a corporate mission: "Wow the customer." Creating a great customer experience became the focus of everyone's job. And the wow factor put Zappos in a class by itself. Now, on the surface, this appears to be a win by "being the best," but in reality it's just like a good Public Toilet. It's there when you need it. Sure, Zappos is the best at customer service, but they are selling commodities. They're selling the same things everyone else is selling. The crux comes where they take away barriers: free shipping, speedier delivery than expected, and free returns. They simply made everything easier...*and* more convenient.

Confusion and Clarity

Be careful not to get too enamored with the books, articles, and stories of Zappo's free socks. A company selling shoes can send its customers free socks all day, but loyalty is not going to result if the transaction process is difficult or time consuming, the product arrives late, it's expensive to ship, or the product can't be returned easily, etcetera. Although Zappos is still on the rise and their model, "wow the consumer," has resulted in a very easy path to purchase, Amazon still provides a more convenient interaction overall.

Winners and Losers

Lululemon, years ago, won the battle of distribution in the yoga market. One of the key players, prAna Living, was founded in 1992 and was an early leader. Relatively close on their heels was Lululemon, a Vancouver-based company entering the yoga market in 1998 with their first retail store in 2000. Realizing quickly there were few established retailers in the yoga wear market, Lululemon capitalized on the difficulty consumers had, at the time, getting access to quality yoga clothing. By pursuing an aggressive retail expansion strategy Lululemon stormed the marketplace and soon owned a majority share of the yoga clothing market, leaving prAna, among others, with little clear and easy access to the yoga consumer.

Prime Takeaway

Loyalty is a result of convenience when:

1. The product is easy to access

2. There are minimal barriers to purchase

3. Product is close and quick at hand

To enact this strategy, knock down every barrier to purchase, typically: distance, time, and money.

Strength of Loyalty Bond

This type of loyalty is by far the weakest of the Five Bonds. There is little depth to the exchange. The smart move is to add to this bond with one or more of the other Bonds of Loyalty and utilize it to augment a bond of greater strength.

Promotional

Consumers suffer from attention deficit disorder. Brand managers may be less attuned to this fact, but any VP of sales is quick to highlight that the end consumer is a fleeting and distracted animal.

The typical strategy for chasing consumer attention comes in two forms: shouting about price and shouting about quality. Price and quality are very important motivating elements; however, in this context, we are talking strictly about commodity marketing. To be specific, we are discussing products that are not distinct: the price is roughly the same, quality is indistinguishable, and the features or ingredients of the given widget are equal. This is the instance when greater or lesser value is not easily discerned. Commodities are what we mostly purchase: toilet paper, cell phones (yes, cell phones), vitamins, etcetera. Typically when buying commodities, even when faced with the classic decision of Pepsi versus Coke, consumers are highly influenced by advertising that pounds the respective brand names into their consciousness and connects a brand with the idea of best price or quality.

In the case where advertising has not created some perceived distinction, consumers end up truly disinterested in which brand they buy so long as they get the best price. And, that often occurs with a coupon in hand.

In this scenario, loyalty is based on presence. How well can Coke keep Coke top of mind? The weaponry employed to win the battle is simple advertising and promotions. Brands spend countless advertising dollars trying to convince the consumer they have a better product (they don't), and when they begin to lose ground with that approach, they resort to offering coupons, discounts, or sweepstakes to cajole the consumer into a purchase. This is famously described as the "Red Ocean" strategy, a bloody environment where market share is bought rather than earned.

Caveat

The largest advertising budget usually wins this game. If you're a late entry, or small player, be prepared to spend lavishly to compete or catch up.

An Example of the Alternative by Jones Soda

Jones Soda became the cola of choice among the snowboarding, surfing, and skating subculture and expanded its distribution and popularity based on a corporate identity of social responsibility and change. They, in fact, started a campaign called "Change Your Soda" as a means to identify with a consumer wanting something different than the mainstream. The ingredients are roughly the same as Coke and Pepsi, but Jones Soda established a niche market based on selling who they are, not what they make. They've effectively non-commoditized their product. They can't compete with the big advertising budgets, and in fact their product is a third more expensive than Coke and Pepsi. While Coke and Pepsi continue to pursue loyalty on a promotional basis, Jones Soda has changed the game, employing a different loyalty strategy (see tribal and ethical below).

Confusion and Clarity

Coke versus Pepsi. Yes, everyone has a preference, and Coke has squeezed out a lead from a market share perspective, but blind taste tests net a 50/50 split. How does one make sense of the consumer's opinion favoring one over the other, when the taste tests bear different results? Coke wins the battle of advertising. They have won and continue to do so; however, if they ever take their foot off the pedal, Pepsi will be sure to rise in market share to usurp the leader. Brand managers will argue it's a case of "better branding;" however, battles for market share among commodities are won by the louder voice, or by who can win on price at the point of purchase. The point of clarity becomes more obvious when a new entry pitches something beyond the product; i.e., creating value beyond the commodity. Jones Soda is the perfect example in the cola market. That's good branding.

Winners and Losers

Remember Jolt Cola? If you're younger than forty, probably not, because Red Bull has taken over the world. The two company's strategic targets were and are the same, and the ingredients mix is in the same ballpark: "All the sugar and twice the caffeine." The difference? Red Bull made a clear commitment to their advertising spend and have kept the pressure on. In certain terms, these types of brands build a following via an intense image-oriented promotions campaign. However, once the advertising dollars wane, there is little to continue the mystique, as there is no real substance to the brand, and they wither and die. Jolt Cola didn't heed that lesson. Founded in 1985, they went bankrupt in 2009.

Prime Takeaway

Loyalty is a result of promotions and advertising when:

1. The product is a commodity

2. Advertising is the key influencer

3. Price wars, discounts and coupons are the default once advertising is saturated

It's an arms race. To win the promotional game, you have to be willing to out gun the competition.

Strength of Loyalty Bond

Weak. The next loudest competitor will up the ante, and if the incumbent can't match, customers will simply move on.

Superior

Loyalty due to a competitive advantage is achieved based on a true distinction that is of value to the consumer, rather than some perceived superiority, like with Coke or Pepsi. We are talking about a measurable win—a better mousetrap. Examples include: Skype's free phone service, Cervelo Bicycles' fastest time trials bikes, and Toyota's most fuel efficient Prius.

Many consumers want the best, and when a brand or product truly is the best, that brand will have the advantage for as long as they can maintain the top spot in their given category. Danger lurks, however, as these are the brands with a target on their backs. As soon as another automobile manufacturer produces a seventy-five-mile-per-gallon sedan, the Prius will simply become a part of history, no longer the model that is propping up Toyota's overall sales. Toyota must understand this threat and work diligently to continue to raise the bar they themselves have set. If not, someone else will (*like Tesla?*). Through the end of 2011 and into 2012, Toyota introduced three new versions of the Prius. One is 100% electric, thus raising the bar.

The pinnacle of this strategy gives us product experiences that border on genius: The Lamborghini P400S Miura is one such example. The history of the Miura is recounted here by "Chris on Cars:"[xx]

> "It all started with an argument between a simple farmer-turned-tractor-manufacturer   named Ferruccio Lamborghini, and the high priest of performance cars, Enzo Ferrari. Lamborghini was a successful businessman and car collector, who owned cars from Alfa Romeo, Lancia, Mercedes, and eventually Ferrari.
>
> "He purchased his first Ferrari in 1958, but was unhappy with both the interior and the clutch. In his opinion, Ferrari built track

cars that were modified for the street, and he became especially annoyed at the amount of time the car required for service. Being the type of person he was, Lamborghini brought his complaints direct to Enzo Ferrari, who arrogantly informed him that the problem was with the driver, not the car, and that, as a tractor manufacturer, Lamborghini, didn't understand real engineering.

"That, according to legend, was when Lamborghini decided to build cars, and, more specifically, cars that were better than Ferrari. The company started by creating Bizzarrini-designed Grand Tourers, which were a hit with the critics but slow sellers in the showroom. Eventually, the designers created a new car, working nights, against Lamborghini's wishes. The car they designed was a two-seat, longitudinally mounted mid-engined car, using a new V12 that merged the engine, transmission, and differential. This design started the trend in high performance sports cars, and became the father of the modern day supercar."

It's all about how you see and understand the world. Lamborghini and Ferrari were steadfast in their respective visions. Lamborghini valued style and curb appeal while Ferrari valued performance. To the casual observer, both made high-performance, iconic, eye-catching cars, but to the fanatic, the two represent divergent philosophies. The beauty is that each philosophy resonates with their respective audience.

To the Lamborghini fan, Ferruccio made the best car. To the Ferrari fan, only Enzo produced the best.

Caveat

Customer loyalty is fleeting in this environment because customers that want the best are always seeking something better. Innovation is the key to their hearts. Being the best requires a steadfast commitment to always winning the established battle. Consumers communicate very efficiently these days, so the advantage goes to the consumer. When there is a better mousetrap available, it doesn't take long for word to spread.

An Example of Defining Quality by BMW

BMW is positioned relative to a very different core purpose than Ferrari. Among potential buyers of a high-end car featuring a relatively sane price point and a pragmatic end use, BMW has seized the position as the best 'driving experience' in an all-around functional automobile. If you're in the market for a high-performance sedan to commute to work, drive to dinner on date night, or zip the kids to lacrosse practice, BMW beats Ferrari. Ferrari is an altogether different driving experience that appeals to an entirely different set of criteria. Per the point, define the criteria of quality from your core principles and then speak specifically to that particular definition.

Confusion and Clarity

A further word about quality: Volvo, Mercedes Benz, and BMW all compete for buyers of automobiles. However, each has achieved a status of "best" by defining quality on their own terms. Volvo—safety. Mercedes Benz—German engineering. BMW—the best driving experience. Each brand appeals to a different sensibility among potential consumers within the overall category of automobile buyers. If it's safety you seek, Volvo is your brand. If you appreciate perfection, buy a Mercedes. If you want the best physical experience behind the wheel (with more than one passenger), buy a BMW. Best can and should be a narrow definition. Quality comes in myriad forms, so be sure it's defined accurately and distinctly per your values. Simply saying you have "high quality" is an exercise in wasted words. Regardless of your category, be certain to define the type of quality your brand represents, and support it with evidence that is clear and overt. If you truly can't claim superiority, then you're fishing with the wrong net.

Winners and Losers

Toyota and General Motors are almost too easy to use as examples here. While GM speaks generally about all of its brands as "high-quality," Toyota gives each brand, sub-brand, and model category particular attributes of quality. Sometimes it's durability, sometimes it's gas mileage, sometimes it's user satisfaction ratings, and sometimes it's value. Each is articulated painstakingly to the target audience. Toyota as an overarching brand generally denotes high quality, but we can only say that as consumers because we understand the detail that underlies that phrase, detail that has been narrowly described and manifested in the user experience of each particular brand, sub-brand, and model.

Prime Takeaway

Loyalty is a result of superiority when:

1. Reputation supersedes claims; i.e., it's common knowledge that the product stands alone

2. The type of quality defined is an obvious advantage for the consumer

3. The provider cannot be replaced: "There is no substitute."

Being the best means innovative thinking, the commitment to fund R&D, and the strategic ability to constantly improve.

Strength of Loyalty Bond

Very strong if the claim of being the best is proven out by the consumer and there is a shared opinion in the marketplace substantiating the claim.

Tribal

We humans all want to be part of something. We long to belong to a tribe, an exclusive club, or a group that represents something we believe in, is cool, or enhances our personal image and status. Being a fan of the Lakers, for example, makes us feel like winners. Riding a Harley Davidson makes us feel badass.

Being part of a group or community goes beyond being the best or looking good. There is a social fabric we as human beings need to be a part of to feel fulfilled. Clubs of every shape and size demonstrate this. The sitcom *Cheers* built a storyline about a diverse group of individuals that shared a common connection via their local bar. The Cubs are often held up as the symbol of futility in professional sports having not won a World Series since 1908, yet they have a rabid fan base that find something beyond just solace in the affinity of their group. Many Brands achieve this same cult following. Harley has capitalized by selling shiny, loud motorcycles. Even though the product itself has been known for poor quality and performance, it's the social network and sense of belonging to a tribe that make the difference.

As long as Harley Davidson stays true to the values established within their tribe, loyalty will ensue. Harley management describes their approach deliberately: "An appropriate and strategically attractive relationship goal is to build best friendships," which they see as "more aligned with the spirit of the brotherhood that defined the company's culture." It is this acknowledgement that keeps Harley customers loyal and the bond powerful.

Caveat

The leader must be authentic. Creating a following is based on a mission, cause, or history. It can happen quickly, but only if the mission or cause is clearly stated and people are moved to follow. If there is no substance behind the words, members will know, and seek their tribe elsewhere.

An Example of Authenticity by Harley Davidson

Harley Davidson was founded in 1905, and although it has had a rocky history throughout, the product line that has remained the consistent performer and definition of the brand has been the "Fat Boy." It harkens back to the early part of the 20th century when Harley became the leading motorcycle manufacturer in the world. It is this single product that most exemplifies the culture and "brotherhood" of the brand.

Confusion and Clarity

Beware of branding agencies that claim they know how to create communities. Communities are created around leaders and those that inspire. Without true leadership inspired by a unique point of view, it's easy to fall into the trap of following rather than leading. The environmental movement is a great example. Patagonia and Seventh Generation were both early leaders in operating based on a respect for the environment. They were both lead by individuals pursuing their own sense of right and wrong. Branding was not the goal. Market share was not the goal. In fact, when these companies started their movements the vast majority of consumers didn't care about environmental responsibility. Today, that's different, and the brands that have followed will have a hard time attracting a tribe only because those brands that follow are by definition members of a movement rather than leaders of a movement. So, be careful to know your place in the world before claiming leadership in an attempt to attract a tribe.

Winners and Losers

Patagonia didn't invent the environmental crisis, but they did create the first outdoor brand that voiced an opinion in its defense. Sure, they were first and foremost a product company, and in many ways part of the problem, but in terms of bonding with an audience, they also defined and lead a movement. They challenged the establishment, upsetting the status quo. This is what creates a tribe, a movement or cause that individuals can align with and rally around. Brands that attempt tribal marketing often fall flat because they aren't defining the movement, they're simply joining an existing movement. Nau, an eco-conscious outdoor clothing brand, is an example of a failed attempt at tribal loyalty. Founded by expatriates from Patagonia, Nau espoused the same beliefs and values as Patagonia. They erred by believing that having those values created the tribe. Actually, *sharing* those values made them a part of Patagonia's tribe.

Prime Takeaway

Loyalty is a result of tribal behavior when:

1. Membership is implied, not required

2. It's a one-of-a-kind, or exclusive, group

3. The community rallies around a cause, leader, or movement

There is no faking the leading of a tribe. It's inherent in the founder or leader of a group, cult, or cause.

Strength of Loyalty Bond

Near unbreakable, if the leader is authentic and the core values are maintained.

Ethical

In this instance, when a brand, organization, or nonprofit is the champion of an ethical cause, customers become advocates because they develop an emotional connection with the brand's core purpose. Brands that elicit advocacy based on ethics provide a value beyond just product quality and experience. This connection is the foundation of loyalty in this instance. Customers see this association as something that makes their world better and that creates satisfaction and motivates them to take action. Customers do want to be part of something bigger than themselves, to help achieve something that they can't necessarily achieve on their own. When this relationship is found, consumers move beyond being casual customers and become advocates.

"Doing the right thing," means maintaining a set of values while competing in the marketplace. Being environmentally, socially, and/or ethically responsible is no easy task, and the choice of how those things manifest is often a very personal one made by the founders. Values are personal and they can be polarizing, as is made obvious in political and religious settings.

There is no doubt that this sort of moral alignment can create loyalty—and, in fact, some brands market specifically to consumer bases whose lifestyles are very strictly lead according to those values. When brands are true to those values as well, a deep connection can occur and last not only a lifetime, but can be passed from generation to generation.

Caveat

Be true to your school. Along with this type of loyalty comes nationalism and deeply held belief systems. Cross those lines, or raise a question of integrity, and the result can be cause for near-instantaneous boycotting. The shaky video camera has brought down more than one company claiming to adhere to ethical values when, in fact, they didn't. Levi's, Abercrombie & Fitch, American Apparel, and J. Crew have all had moments when purported values oriented integrity were brought into question.

An Example of Doing the Right Thing

Officially, Jedidiah "is a humanitarian-based apparel brand aspiring to cultivate change, one garment at a time." Their mission is to use the sales of their clothing line to provide care, support, and financial resources to those in need. When a mission is as deeply committed as this, a tangible connection between "What you do" and "Why you do it" needs to be ever-present. If there is too great of a disconnection then the relative importance of doing the right thing fades.

Jedidiah connects purpose with product at nearly every touch point. In fact, many of their products have an end purpose. They tie product development with end causes. Buy this shirt, support this cause. They connect the dots, articulate their purpose clearly, and are building a fan base because of it. Powerful stuff.

Confusion and Clarity

Operating with a triple bottom line, where environmental, social, and ethical responsibility is on par with financial responsibility, creates a natural tension and inevitable compromise. However, compromises do not undermine the intention or the eventual realization of potential solutions. As technologies evolve and consumers further grasp the importance of the triple bottom line, new opportunities present themselves.

Winners and Losers

Flor is the brand name under which Ray Anderson marketed his modular carpet products. Realizing his company was plundering the planet with its dependency on fossil fuels, Anderson bet his company on doing the right thing. He described the challenge as "climbing Mount Sustainability," and since adopting his vision of a sustainable business, the company has realized substantial decreases in greenhouse gas production, fossil fuel consumption, water usage, and landfill waste—all while doubling its earnings. On the flip side, American Apparel claimed to be an advocate of human rights, celebrating their product was "Made in America." The relatively empty statements ultimately blew up in their face as the company was exposed as having "a downtown textile factory straight out of the forties," and is also at the top of many women's rights activists' lists regarding their objectification of women. This is obviously an extreme example, but American Apparel had been a huge success story financially up until just a few years ago, hinging much of their success on marketing messages based on a new ethical standard for American textile manufacturers. Lesson learned: ethics go hand-in-hand with integrity.

Prime Takeaway

Loyalty is a result of ethics when:

1. There is a clear cause that the organization promotes

2. The company operates with a double or triple bottom line (See SEER or B Corp)

3. The brand's consumer is part of the solution

There must be a clear and present link between the values that drive the organization and the customer's experience.

Strength of Loyalty Bond

Very powerful and hard to disrupt by any other brand than the brand itself.

Conclusion

Steve Jobs is worth quoting at this juncture because of his principles. Upon his return to Apple in 1997, Jobs hired Chiat Day, and together they devised the seminal advertising campaign, "Think Different." In his presentation announcing the campaign, Jobs noted, "It's not about talking about speeds and fees," and "it's not to talk about why we're better than Windows." In that talk he was referring to the two approaches available to every marketer, one is steeped in transcendent purpose, the other focused on features and benefits.

The features and benefits approach is well-worn by lots of brands beyond those that suffer the eventual demise illustrated by Eddie Bauer. It's been written about endlessly in strategic marketing books, conferences, and myriad classroom settings, and it comes in lots of different shapes and forms, including: "Blue Ocean" strategies and "Red Ocean" strategies, "Cost," "Differentiation," and "Focus" strategies, and "Innovation" and "Technology" strategies.

All of these features and benefits approaches are varying attempts to carve out a niche that somehow distinguishes the product or service as "the best." We have better technology, we're the first, we are unique, or we are less expensive, and so on and so forth. Those that pursue this features and benefits approach, this "speeds and fees" approach, desperately try to convince their constituencies and themselves that their products are the most worthy. Unfortunately, these strategies in total do not lead to long-term sustainable advantage. Understanding the cognitive processes at work within the minds of consumers enlightens strategies beyond features and benefits. Consumers need stuff. We want stuff and we need stuff based on our very different experiences, beliefs, life circumstances, finances, and mental constructs; it is these collective perspectives that create the point of view from which we determine the value of said stuff. Our cognitive processes determine value, or the worth of things.

**"Knowledge is the
process of piling up
facts, wisdom lies in their
simplification."**

MARTIN H. FISCHER

CHAPTER NINE

Grow Your Own Apple

Now our work is to illustrate the pragmatic process for implementing the concepts I've outlined in this book—and when done right, it is, indeed, a process. What follows are the steps to creating an operational Brand Ecosystem, including the Customer Activation Cycle and Story Universe.

Architecting loyalty begins with understanding how your core customers become your core customers in the first place, and then creating the tools to manage the relationship on a day-to-day basis. In this chapter I will illustrate the construction of a fictitious brand's Brand Ecosystem.

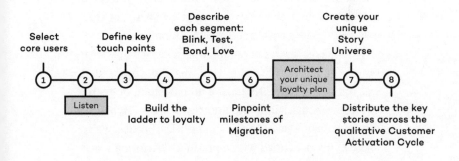

1) Select Core Audience Members

The first step in the process of constructing your particular Customer Activation Cycle is to speak with your core users. As with usability testing, only a small number of representative interviews are required because it is only the commonly held beliefs and key milestone experiences among *all* users that are important. Interviewing ten to twenty of your most loyal customers will suffice. A larger sample of user interviews would yield only slightly varying results. Once the interviews are complete, the process is to cull the entirety of the interview results for common experiences, touch points, milestone experiences, communications, and product interactions. The entirety of this information collected becomes a stream-of-consciousness document, which then serves as the data set to construct the Customer Activation Cycle.

2) Listen

How many times have you been asked by a company to tell them what you think of their product, how you came to be a customer, the story of your relationship, or your own story? Sadly, this isn't likely to happen.

We all have stories about our relationships with brands: what they did right, what they did wrong, what was unusual or exceptional. We all have told, or heard, stories of remarkable experiences with all types of different businesses, charities, or political parties. We've all been overwhelmed with a product's performance or underwhelmed with a restaurant's service. Regardless of the circumstance, we've all got great stories to tell.

The reason we don't get to tell our stories is because most of the people in charge simply don't know their intrinsic value, so they don't ask. As social media creeps more and more into the dialog between consumers and brands, brand managers, and CEOs are becoming increasingly excited about their "customer engagement" practices and the concept of transparency. Social media is a very cursory view of the intimacy of true listening. Company blogs, Facebook pages, surveys, focus groups, and feedback sites like Yelp and TripAdvisor may seem like opportunities for customers to speak their minds, to let their voices shine, but the reality is that this type of feedback is disconnected from the consumer's overall experience. These are singular interactions, not the totality of the experience. Asking for a product review may reveal detailed flaws or positive performance characteristics, but it's just one touch point. It's not the thread in a woven story. Sitting with a customer and truly listening to their journey and experiences interacting with your brand, however, bolsters the bond between users and your brand by uncovering the truth about your brand's successes and failures. It's more than simply knowing the good and the bad, it's about unearthing the consumer's beliefs: their values, prejudices, and preconceived notions about the circumstances that surround your brand and their life. Most importantly, there is opportunity to discover the cognitive processes that are driving their motivations and needs. The quest is to understand what they believe and how they understand your brand. Just a handful of these conversations can unearth the most valuable information.

Stories are an essential part of being human. We communicate most powerfully through stories. They are our most effective method of transferring information, explaining difficult concepts, imparting heartfelt beliefs, and inspiring action.

Brands are all about the stories that surround them. Sometimes it's the stories that brands tell, and sometimes it's the stories that customers, fans, and detractors tell about brands. Either way, we as a consuming public piece together what we know about the world by the stories that we hear, read, see, and experience for ourselves.

The critical revelation is that customers of brands have unique experiences that they carry with them that are a thread of a common story, which when woven together captures the essence of the brand. Not necessarily the brand mission or marketing message, but the meaning the brand has in the lives of its customers.

First Catalog Meeting

One of the first days in my new job at Patagonia as the Sailing Product Team Leader, I attended the fall catalog meeting to represent my category of product and lend my "expert" opinion to the overall storyline of the catalog. This mostly meant keeping my mouth shut. At the time, the main books were mailed only four times a year. There were also specialty catalogs that were distributed into more niche segments: a kids' book, a sailing book, sometimes fly-fishing books, mountain books, mid-season books, etcetera. But the smaller books were more like pet projects and themed to give a bit more voice to the categories that required further space, or categories that simply didn't warrant space in the seasonal main books.

One of the first people I met when getting my orientation was Hal Arneson. Hal was the head of the creative services department. He was the shepherd of the brand, a visual fellow, and a great writer. He was calm in general and downright solemn when it came to his responsibility for the guardrails of the company identity. He was a surfer and a fly-fishermen, he loved to camp and be outside, and he was a generally sweet soul. No one, in my estimation, more embodied the Patagonia brand, and no one articulated it or captured it visually better than Hal. As I walked into that first meeting in the conference room on the second floor of the creative services department, I was distinctly aware that I was walking into the environment where the coffee table catalogs that I'd been reading the majority of my adult life were created. There were probably fifteen to twenty people in the meeting at any given time. Product marketers like myself, copywriters, photo editors, merchants, visual designers, the lead catalog designer, the head of the catalog, and of course Hal. The meeting began shortly after lunch and ran until early evening. There was an ice bucket for the essentials, and bottles of water and beer. The pages of the preliminary layout were pinned to the walls and everyone had their own printed version in front of them, augmented with financial projections and inventory counts of the suggested product. There was palpable tension between Hal's immediate reports, the "creatives,"—the folks responsible for the brand storytelling—and the catalog folks responsible for circulation and sales, and, of course, the product marketers vying for representation and space on the pages. Lots of agendas, but limited space. Ultimately, it was Hal's responsibility to make it all come together into one cohesive storyline, with just the right mix of product, visual inspiration, story, and mission-related diatribe somehow thematically unified and financially feasible. It costs lots of money to produce and distribute a consumer catalog. Selling stuff is the necessary evil. Inspiring a community is the mission. Promote too much by cramming the pages with product, or promote too little by spending all of the real estate on imagery and story, and the magic of the best performing product catalog in the industry is lost. The book turns into just another piece of junk mail. Get it right and it's a cherished heirloom.

Over the four or so hours that I mostly just observed and listened, I got the quintessential lesson in the implementation of core principles. Twenty or so people, all with particular jobs to do and associated agendas, made arguments justifying this or that, from which product should be put on the opening spread, to how many colors of Snap-T's to feature, to what image should grace the cover. Myriad questions accompanied by myriad opinions. Sitting and watching the process was mind-boggling. It was my first catalog meeting. I couldn't help thinking of the numbers of catalogs I'd perused in my day, probably spanning close to twenty years reaching back to my teens, and how this process netted such remarkable consistency of message. Not only consistency of message, but awe-inspiring copy, photography, storytelling, and innovative product. This book lead a movement, created a tribe of people wholeheartedly committed to a shared cause. It inspired people to go outside and live dreams. How could this collective of competing agendas net decades of iconic catalogs? Catalogs people saved like *National Geographic* magazines or *Surfers Journal*s, stacked in a special place in their homes, protected for future generations. I was mesmerized at how seemingly ad hoc it all seemed and struggled to understand how this was the process that was at the root of this historically significant signature piece of Patagonia's brand landscape.

But there it was. One voice in the room driven not by a personal agenda, a particular role in the organization, or a need to win an argument, one voice driven by the core purpose of the organization as a whole. Hal never had an opinion, never spoke of his own ideas. He was more than a sentinel. His active participation kept everyone immersed in the core purpose of the company and in the organizing principles of the company. The example that best captures this challenge is the selection of the image on the cover. This is a defining moment. The images that make it into final consideration are always remarkable in context and composition, but an image that evokes the character of the organization is rare. "I can't describe it, but when I see it I know." There's reverence, man's place in the cosmos (not an overstatement), the fragility of nature, communion, not intelligence but intellect, humor, joy, love, and awe. The true essence of a thing must be held closely in principle for the thing to manifest its meaning. That was Hal's job. That was my first moment seeing principle enacted fully and openly.

"Can Clothing Have a Soul?"

This important principle was made obvious to us at Patagonia in the midst of a qualitative study we conducted regarding how fans of Patagonia became fans. We interviewed customers one at a time. A small team of interviewers (see: Kazaks, Alex, and Ayr Muir-Harmony. Customer Life Cycle Study. Patagonia, 2004.)

went to our retail stores, called people on the phone, and had customers come and visit our home offices. In each instance the interviews were loosely structured, focused on that individual's experience of being a Patagonia customer. The interviewers had no rigid agenda other than to listen and record stories. What followed was an exhaustive compilation of notes, videos, and statistics by two Harvard interns who spent their summer at Patagonia helping us study how and why Patagonia fans became Patagonia fans.

The results contributed to numerous initiatives inside the walls at Patagonia—most importantly, helping us organize our own marketing efforts across five different sales channels. For me, the impact was life-changing. It started me down the path of studying how brands, products, services, nonprofits, political parties, and educational institutions play meaningful roles in individuals' lives.

One of the most intriguing questions asked during the study was, "Can a piece of clothing have a soul?" Long-term, loyal Patagonia customers answered unanimously: "Yes." Short-term product buyers had a difficult time even interpreting the question. For every individual that answered in the affirmative there was a story associated with the answer. These stories recounted the experiences that deeply affected those people's lives, and they related the clothing directly to those experiences. It was the crux of why customers connected to the brand.

Marketing and branding experts talk a lot about quality and service, and the impact of creative and positioning. That summer, I realized Patagonia was providing customers much more than a high-quality product and a message about the environment. We were sharing life-altering experiences. We were connecting with people in profound ways. The clothing was such an intimate part of those experiences that the items themselves took on meaning in the lives of the user. They became living, breathing partners in the experiences, in many cases making those experiences possible. Each experience captured in stories that live on forever.

Everyone Has a Story

The stories vary from amazing to mundane.

A professional fisherman, Bering Strait sort of guy, went missing overboard. So the legend goes, he was pulled from the drink, hypothermic and comatose. His shipmates and rescuers proceeded to strip his wet gear in preparation for getting him into a sleeping bag with another warm body, as is the common practice for victims of hypothermia. In the midst of his shipmates slicing away at his Patagonia Capilene long underwear, he shocked everyone by bolting upright and grabbing their scissor-wielding hands with a near death grip. Deterred after several attempts to get the freezing, wet gear off of the fisherman, they simply put him in the sleeping bag still wearing his soaking wet Capilene. As he slowly warmed from the reflective heat of the other person snuggled next to him, he gained consciousness and full function. Disaster averted, but the rescuers were still curious, why had the fisherman been so intent on stopping them from cutting off his Capilene when, in every other manner of speaking, he was gone to the world? The fisherman told them, "I knew, had you cut off my Capilene, I would have died."

Then there was the story of a young mother of two boys, ages eight and ten. She told of a simple miscommunication that initiated her path to loyalty. The woman and her husband had a busy Saturday planned with family events. The Dad was headed to the beach for a day of various water activities with their two boys. Mom was headed out on some errands with plans to rendezvous later at the beach to dress and clean up before heading to a family birthday party for Grandpa. Not necessarily the stuff of legend so far. At the end of the day, the trio at the beach were no sight for sore eyes. The boys, both dressed in sun protective shirts and pants by Patagonia, were a mess: soaking wet, salty, sandy, and layered with sweat. Disheveled was putting it lightly. Mom was not deterred because she knew Dad had the change of clothes she'd left for them in the living room the night before, and with a quick wash up and change they'd be good to go. Dad wasn't worried because he figured his wife always had the goods to get the kids cleaned up and looking presentable. *Oops*. Neither Mom or Dad had actually brought the clothes for the party. With this new knowledge in hand, and the clock ticking, was it possible to do an hour round trip all the way home? No way. The remedy? Strip the boys down, lay the clothes over the dashboard of the car and truck, turn the heaters on maximum and hope for the best. True to form, Patagonia's design principles manifested in dry gear by the end of the trek to the restaurant. The boys quickly got dressed, fluffed their hair and brushed off the remaining residue of dirt and salt, and remarkably both kids looked no worse for wear. Success. The mom's comment, "Had it not been for Patagonia, that would have been a disaster." A small but meaningful battle that was good to win.

We have story after story like this. Customers start superficially. The depth of understanding evolves throughout the conversation. It's easy to think these stories are all about product performance, but they're not. What surrounds them and what's discovered through listening is context. In Patagonia's case, customers live with the product a long time before they have a milestone experience like those recounted above, or they learn over years and years of use that the product is durable beyond expectation. They slowly appreciate the classic styling, recognizing that ten years later they can still wear that fleece hidden in the back of the closet. Some customers have a product issue and discover that, regardless of the reason, Patagonia stands behind the product with their Ironclad Guarantee. And, finally, through many disparate interactions, customers come to understand more and more about the philosophies and values Patagonia holds dear about the environment, innovation, and culture: Patagonia provided one of the first onsite day care centers for workers' children, used reclaimed materials as foundational materials in their retail stores, and fought to pioneer the use of organic cotton across the product line. These discoveries don't happen overnight. They're not encapsulated in a tagline. And the experiences are not linear, nor are they the same for every customer. Over time, the milestones that meaningfully impart these understandings are common. These are the keys to building a relationship.

Customers eventually come to understand why the product performs the way it does, they come to know there are design principles that make it so, that there is a philosophy behind the design principles that make the production process as environmentally friendly as possible, and in the end they learn that Patagonia is doing things the way they too would want things done. They come to understand that they have a shared belief about integrity, environmental quality, and innovation. The brand and the customer align. At the moment of clarity about aligned and shared beliefs, the customer and the brand fuse. This is fanatical loyalty.

Sharing these stories in this book is great fodder to prove a point, but the real opportunity for you is in delving into the stories your customers hold about your brand, your service, or your cause.

After this story-gathering phase, we start to construct the Customer Activation Cycle.

Asking the Right Questions

Learning how to ask the right questions is probably the most interesting and critical aspect of strategically understanding the elements that drive fandom. Listening to stories is also the way to learn about what is inside the hearts and minds of the customers.

Two words of caution: this is not an exercise in writing personas, and it's not about you.

As much as the creative and marketing worlds continue to promote their love affair with penning personas, there is likely nothing that undermines a clear understanding of customer needs, beliefs, and perceptions more than personas. In some cases brand creatives will pen as many as fifteen different personas, when, in reality, as we've learned, among those many varying physically unique attributes, there is *one* commonly held belief that resonates with all of them. It's the discovery of these overwhelming nuggets of idealism that matters most. To demonstrate the point, the following quotes are from a variety of customers interviewed specifically about their experience with the high-end, botanical skin care brand, Naturopathica.

> "I had baby a year ago, my skin went crazy. Total unpredictability, so dry. I randomly broke out, throughout the month. They were severe too. Been looking for the solution to my problem for about a year."

> "I've always done yoga, and exercised regularly, plus I'm a vegetarian. That's why it was so frustrating that my skin was breaking out."

> "Not really, you'd be surprised how rare facial care comes up as a topic among fifty-plus-year-old men."

Three quotes, three entirely different people. In fact, if we were to pen personas from these three customers that were representative loyal cheerleaders of this brand we would have: Sally, young mother; Veronica, new age health enthusiast and vegetarian activist; and Bob, fifty years plus, father, businessman, and weekend warrior. Pretty tough to pin down a brand position for this crew; pretty easy to define their common need, which in this case is a solution for nagging skin problems. A solution that resides exclusively in botanical-based, organic, topical skin tinctures and remedies. Remarkably, this brand's core customers are not necessarily health or beauty seekers. They are remedy seekers. People with particular problems with their skin that their dermatologists, doctors, estheticians, mothers and fathers, friends, and co-workers could not help them find solutions for. And they had hunted high and low for a solution. They came from varying economic circumstances, demographics, geo-graphic locales, and—although primarily female—there were plenty of men enamored with the brand as well. Further digging among cheerleaders of this brand uncovered a common belief they held, and, in fact, the founder of the brand held as well, that living close to nature was a base principle. They as individuals sought out a more holistic lifestyle to contribute to their wellbeing and made significant life changes in order to realize that goal. We found this to be driven by a commonly held belief in observing nature.

> "For me this conjures an idea of staying true to our roots as human beings...less processed, less of a dramatic transformation from something's original state. Unbleached, untreated, more authentic material...something less designed."

Insights such as this, that turn out to be commonly held values among customers, cannot be known without the process of deep interviewing and objective listening. There's not a survey on the planet that will get to this depth of meaning. This is where the long-term relationship of cheerleaders, long-term sustainable customers, resides.

Beliefs, Values, and Needs Rather Than Personas and Demographics

The second caveat is that it's not all about you. The tricky part of listening is refraining from inserting your own opinion or influence into what you hear. You may have a lot invested in your brand identity, and you may have a strongly held opinion about what will work, or what should work. If experience has taught us anything, it's that within the process of listening to customers tell their stories, be cautious about what you want to hear. Instead, focus on learning what your customers have to say. After all, it's their life you're trying to understand.

Internally, Naturopathica held two strong opinions about the value the brand represented in the marketplace. One opinion was that Naturopathica was truly an innovative product company, with some of the most effective remedies, tinctures, and treatments on the market, authentically created from natural ingredients. Another closely held opinion was that highly affluent beauty and luxury seekers would be the ideal target audience. Customers' experience of the product confirmed the first internal opinion about innovation; however, the users of the product felt very much that the luxury brand identity Naturopathica sought was misleading and distracting from the overall good that the company could achieve. In fact, consensus among consumers was that Naturopathica was somehow not being true to its roots and founding principles by focusing on beauty and not enough about health, wellness, natural remedies, and organic ingredients all leading to beauty as a byproduct of living a healthy lifestyle close to nature. These were the values the customer's held. They wanted those to be the values that Naturopathica held as well.

Although the product was incredibly well received, this message about focusing on remedies, focusing on the authentic origins and intentions behind the product, was a very difficult thing for the internal leadership to reconcile. Ultimately, they set aside their own agenda about capitalizing on the beauty market and trusted that their values would be enough, and listened to what was resonating between what they truly believed and what the consumer also believed. The net result was the confidence internally to present the brand in the light that its founder had pursued in its formation.

3) Define Key Touch Points

Two laddering exercises follow. The first is the Affinity Ladder. The Affinity Ladder identifies key points of customer contact and what each means relative to the job they perform in the core consumer's life. This is the collection of every meaningful touch point in the provider/user relationship. Not every touch point, just those that have an impact. Each touch point is then described in terms of how the user perceives "What It Is" and "What It Does." It's critical to note, these interpretations of what each touch point is and what each does is through the eyes of the user, such that nuances of the user experience begin to take shape. What might be a common description to your design team, product team, or marketing manager may take on an entirely new interpretation through the experience of the user.

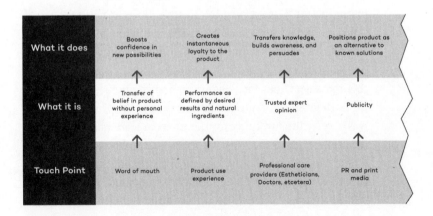

Figure 1: Affinity Ladder

4) Build the Ladder to Loyalty

The second ladder exercise is the Loyalty Ladder. The Loyalty Ladder demonstrates the steps in the provider/ user relationship that lead to loyalty, how each step occurs, and the associated contribution to advancing the consumer toward loyalty.

Again, each event, this time in sequence, is defined in the user's terms and perspective. Each step in the path to loyalty is described in terms of "How it Happens" and in terms of "What It Means" in the user's life. Objectivity is key in mapping these experiences and tracking the definitions provided by the user via interviews. While the tendency is to interpret for the user, or massage the truth, if the process is to yield value, you must practice objectivity.

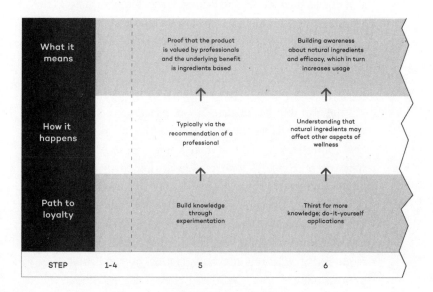

Figure 2: Loyalty Ladder

5) Describe Each Segment by the User's Most Important Cognitive Process

Throughout this process of interviewing, culling, and laddering, bubbling to the surface are four distinct states of consciousness relative to the beliefs and impressions the core user has along their path to loyalty and their path to understanding, from blink to test to bond to love.

Blink...

Captures the vast population of potential users that harbor a desire, need, and set of values that align with you as the provider of the service or product. These are prospects. They are the largest segment and represent total potential. This is anyone and everyone that ultimately believes what you do, but has yet to be introduced. Describing them must be in terms of how they describe their mental state and their need state.

See Figure 3: Blink: First Segment Description: Prospects

Test...

Is it the user that has made a first transaction, meaning they've tried the product or service based on their first impression of how it may serve them? At this stage there are key performance attributes that the product or service must deliver. Again, this is entirely subjective and interpreted through the eyes of the user. These are casual users. Identifying very specifically the performance characteristics they seek is the requirement. It is this they are "testing" to see if first impressions are true. If validated, they are then primed to move to the next stage of loyalty. This is fleeting and typically based entirely on product and service quality as defined by the user.

See Figure 3: Test: Second Segment Description: Casuals

Bond...

Things are getting serious now. The user can be described in more meaningful terms. This description is no longer about surface impressions and quality. This segment must be described by their beliefs relative to the offer. What is it these customers have bought into that looms larger in their personal core values and ethics? Here is likely where either tribal or ethical loyalty takes root. Describing this segment is describing the bond on which the long-term relationship will be based.

See Figure 3: Bond: Third Segment Description: Loyalists

Love...

The Holy Grail. This segment description is about lifestyle. Core beliefs dictate aesthetic, quality, causes, and the most distinguishing characteristics of your customer. This is your core customer. These are the people that most represent the organization's founding principles: the passion, the driving inspiration, and identity of the brand. This segment description is the walking, talking embodiment of the brand identity: your cheerleaders, the people that will advocate strongly for your product or service.

See Figure 3: Love: The Final Segment Description: Cheerleaders

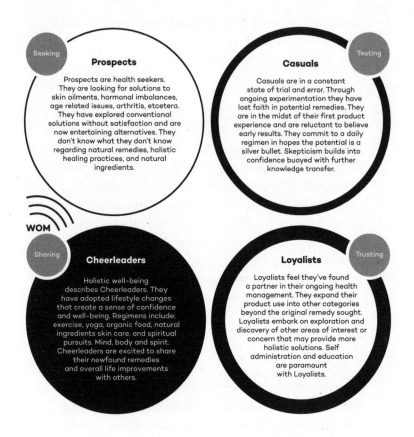

Figure 3: Blink to Test to Bond to Love

6) Pinpoint Milestones of Migration

It's now the point in the process to put into words the singular influence that migrates the user from one segment to the next. What moves or persuades an individual user to move from blink to test to bond to love. The critical moments, bits of information, product experiences, communications, or service revelations do. These are conclusive brand architecture milestones that either move the user to a further state of loyalty, or show how loyalty is disrupted.

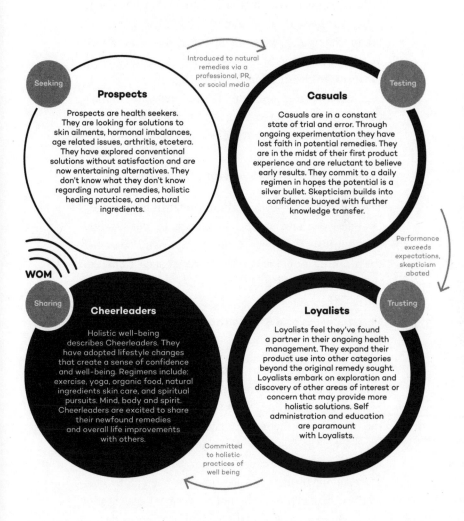

Prospects · Seeking

Introduced to natural remedies via a professional, PR, or social media

Prospects are health seekers. They are looking for solutions to skin ailments, hormonal imbalances, age related issues, arthritis, etcetera. They have explored conventional solutions without satisfaction and are now entertaining alternatives. They don't know what they don't know regarding natural remedies, holistic healing practices, and natural ingredients.

Casuals · Testing

Casuals are in a constant state of trial and error. Through ongoing experimentation they have lost faith in potential remedies. They are in the midst of their first product experience and are reluctant to believe early results. They commit to a daily regimen in hopes the potential is a silver bullet. Skepticism builds into confidence buoyed with further knowledge transfer.

Performance exceeds expectations, skepticism abated

WOM

Cheerleaders · Sharing

Holistic well-being describes Cheerleaders. They have adopted lifestyle changes that create a sense of confidence and well-being. Regimens include: exercise, yoga, organic food, natural ingredients skin care, and spiritual pursuits. Mind, body, and spirit. Cheerleaders are excited to share their newfound remedies and overall life improvements with others.

Loyalists · Trusting

Loyalists feel they've found a partner in their ongoing health management. They expand their product use into other categories beyond the original remedy sought. Loyalists embark on exploration and discovery of other areas of interest or concern that may provide more holistic solutions. Self administration and education are paramount with Loyalists.

Committed to holistic practices of well being

Figure 4: Migration Moments

Architecting Your Unique Loyalty Plan

We've finally arrived. With a full understanding of the path your most loyal customers take to become active brand champions, you can now put the structure in place to repeat that process of attracting and migrating prospects to cheerleaders again and again.

Just two steps remain: 1) Creating your brand's unique Story Universe; and, 2) distributing these key stories across the qualitative Customer Activation Cycle.

7) Creating Your Unique Story Universe:

The true value and power of a brand's identity is leveraged by relatively few. It is a challenge to consistently communicate the values the brand represents such that the meaning is obvious to the consumer at each stage of the Customer Activation Cycle.

The Artifacts and Stories that Make the Story Universe

Moments in time, events, historical milestones, battles, championships, and cultural movements, are all defined by the stories leading up to them, the stories relating the occurrences themselves, and the stories told about them after the fact. The stories often accumulate over time, evolve, and are consistently embellished. They are passed along by firsthand accounts and even more often by those one, two, or more times removed. Regardless of the medium, regardless of the credibility of those relaying the story, regardless of how many degrees of separation from the eyewitness, the truth is, stories are pieced together through the interpretive lens of the recipient. In the case of brands, that means the consumer.

Brands are complex. They are made up of product, service, values, performance, geography, reputation, visual stimuli, imagery, and personality. And all of these attributes are expressed, good or bad, through hands-on experiences and rumor: what I collectively call stories. The landscape is vast, even for tiny brands that service just handfuls of clients. For the corner coffee shop, it is where its located, the pleasantness of the help, the cleanliness of the bathrooms, the décor, the ambiance, and the variety of product and quality of the product. All make fodder for stories, and each and every item is a potential story unto itself. It is the collection of these stories that defines the brand, creates context for judgment, and enables consumers to discern. The intricacy of this tapestry is what customers draw conclusions from that precedes and leads them to creating a bond or not.

Every brand has its own footprint, big or small; brands vast with history and breadth of stories, or brands anew able to relate to only a smattering of topical variety. The Story Universe is an accounting of the history, the topics of interest, the areas of importance, and the values that have relevance to the brand's reason for being—its core organizing principle. Every element that makes a brand unique should be accounted for in the Story Universe. Every aspect of the brand that can be explained to, or shared with, an end consumer that somehow expresses the brand's core purpose must be charted, captured, mapped.

The Story Universe is the entirety of the critical, defining artifacts that emanate from the brand's core purpose, artifacts that exist solely because of the brand's reason for being. It captures the value set and the organizing principles that drive the end customer experience and the product or service offering to which the consumer responds. It is organized as a universe, expanding outward from a central event. As the universe expands there is always a tether from the edge of the universe back to that defining, initial inspiration— the founding principle of the organization. Therefore, the essence of that founding principle is manifest in each and every peripheral artifact or story such that, regardless of the number of these artifacts or stories a customer interacts with, they are getting the core message in some dosage. Over time, with more and more diverse experiences and exposure, the consumer slowly understands the core purpose, the founding principle, and the organizing principle. They draw conclusions about the values that drive the organization as a whole. It is these values the consumer eventually bonds with based on their own beliefs and held values.

Therefore, to construct a Story Universe is to take control of the totality of possible experiences your end consumer has when in relationship with your brand. It is only when you've clearly acknowledged and committed to a core reason for being, an organizing principle, that you can define the stories and artifacts that matter to you. Only then can you decide what type of quality you define as yours, or what service means to you, or the context that defines the actual business model. Only then can you map the totality of your Story Universe such that you see the balance across all of the possibilities your customer may encounter with your brand.

Once you have charted your universe, once each and every artifact is accounted for, then you have a powerful tool to manage your customer's experience. Now you have a means to measure and direct the development of the communications, messages, and content that your customers interact with. In an active state, the Story Universe acts as a heat map, tracking the involvement of your customer with your brand experience. If you're only telling them one or two stories, then they won't understand vast pockets of your universe that may be mission-critical to their knowledge of your brand, aspects that may cause them to bond or not. By managing your customer's experience through the Story Universe, you are ensuring they glean your purpose in every context.

Understanding the inspiration that drives the organization as a whole motivates consumer behavior. By knowing your purpose through piecing together seemingly disparate experiences and bits of information and knowledge, customers become armed with the context to make deeper and deeper commitments. This is absolutely how we can predict a successful relationship between your customer and your brand, because there are specific people in the world that believe what you believe, that want what you do specifically the way you do it. It's not about targeting a customer base, it's about clearly articulating your perspective and then sharing the nuances of that perspective so that your customer, who is looking for the product or service that you provide, will understand your worldview. If there's agreement on that worldview, and your product or service performs and meets expectations then you'll have an aligned platform upon which to forge a long-term sustainable relationship with that person as your customer.

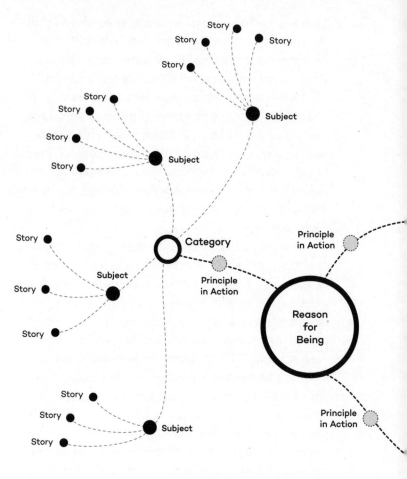
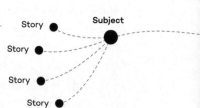

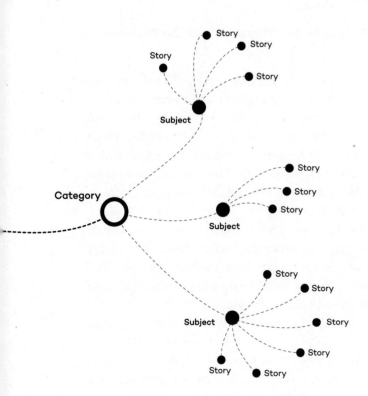

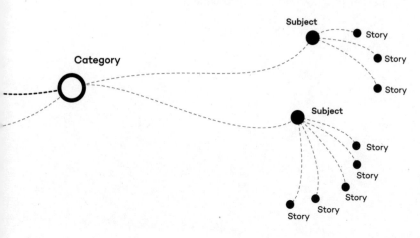

8) Distribute Key Stories Across the Customer Activation Cycle

The Story Universe is the tool by which the greatest efficiency is achieved in indoctrinating new customers. Now, in partnership with the Customer Activation Cycle, we have the entirety of the Brand Ecosystem defined. The final step is to identify the organization's goal for each segment of the Customer Activation Cycle relative to the key attribute of each user segment. Then, devise the process by which that goal will be realized. Assign the primary merchandise most appropriate for each segment. And finally, capture the most important message or experience from the Story Universe that must be communicated or take place to migrate the user from one segment to the next.

Once the Customer Activation Cycle is enabled, each part of the organization can operate from the same organizing principles. Long-term, sustainable loyalty is essentially a result of a rhythm of implementation, measuring migration, and refinement.

Attributes
Seeking healthier ways to live. Specifically looking to resolve a current skin ailment

Goal
Expose to alternative solutions, knowledge, education about natural ingredients and their efficacy

Process
Publish information about ingredients based solutions through social media, articles and video. Create a knowledge base and distribute via PR

Attributes
Skeptical of any solution or recommendation

Goal
Gain confidence in a single remedy

Process
Use vicarious storytelling, testimonials, in order to build confidence, demonstrate efficacy. Provide knowledge about botanical properties as applied to health and wellness

Introduced to natural remedies via a professional, PR, or social media

Seeking

Prospects

Prospects are health seekers. They are looking for solutions to skin ailments, hormonal imbalances, age related issues, arthritis, etcetera. They have explored conventional solutions without satisfaction and are now entertaining alternatives. They don't know what they don't know regarding natural remedies, holistic healing practices, and natural ingredients.

Testing

Casuals

Casuals are in a constant state of trial and error. Through ongoing experimentation they have lost faith in potential remedies. They are in the midst of their first product experience and are reluctant to believe early results. They commit to a daily regimen in hopes the potential is a silver bullet. Skepticism builds into confidence buoyed with further knowledge transfer.

Performance exceeds expectations, skepticism abated

WOM

Sharing

Cheerleaders

Holistic well-being describes Cheerleaders. They have adopted lifestyle changes that create a sense of confidence and well-being. Regimens include: exercise, yoga, organic food, natural ingredients skin care, and spiritual pursuits. Mind, body and spirit. Cheerleaders are excited to share their newfound remedies and overall life improvements with others.

Trusting

Loyalists

Loyalists feel they've found a partner in their ongoing health management. They expand their product use into other categories beyond the original remedy sought. Loyalists embark on exploration and discovery of other areas of interest or concern that may provide more holistic solutions. Self administration and education are paramount with Loyalists.

Committed to holistic practices of well being

Attributes
Steeped in a continuing practice. Confident in newfound holistic wellness providers

Goal
Employ as evangelists to affect circle of influence

Process
Arm with access to information, expertise, ongoing education and expanded product offerings

Attributes
Expanding knowledge and confidence in natural remedies, nature based ingredients

Goal
Assist in furthering knowledge, transfer to other applications and categories of product

Process
Provide access to expert opinion, how-to-guides for do-it-yourself applications, and shared knowledge via social media

Figure 5: The Qualitative Customer Activation Cycle

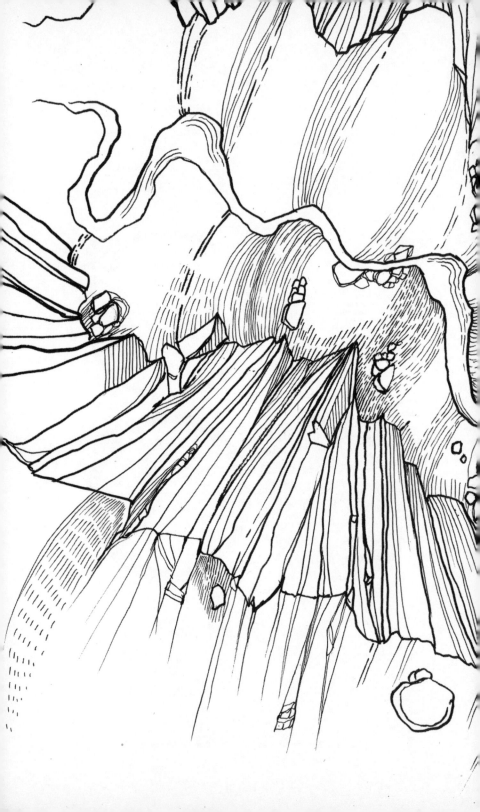

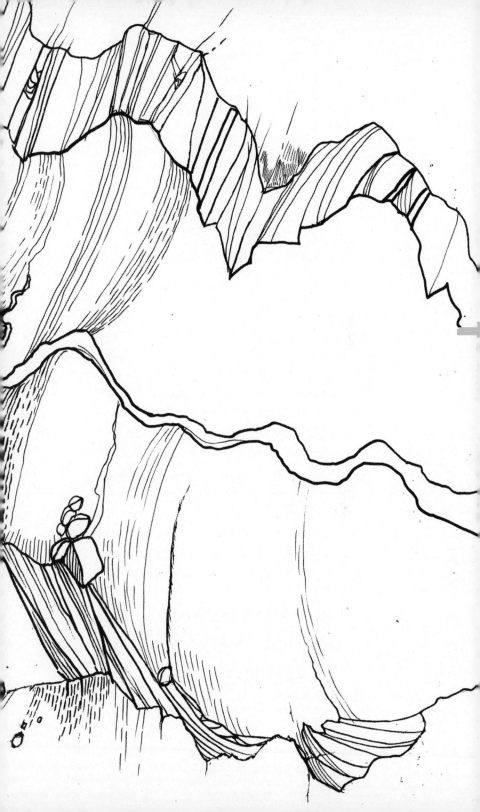

"Anyway, I keep picturing all these little kids playing some game in this big field of rye and all. Thousands of little kids, and nobody's around—nobody big, I mean—except me. And I'm standing on the edge of some crazy cliff. What I have to do, I have to catch everybody if they start to go over the cliff—I mean if they're running and they don't look where they're going I have to come out from somewhere and catch them.

"I know it's crazy, but that's the only thing I'd really like to be."

J. D. SALINGER, *THE CATCHER IN THE RYE*

CHAPTER TEN

Standing on the Edge of Some Crazy Cliff

It's no easy or obvious task to embark on a grand mission of change. I didn't set out to write a book about the environment, nor did I intend to become an authority on how great companies engender great customers. I certainly didn't think those two ideas would be so intimately connected. I started out by simply helping companies grow and secure a profit.

The more I worked, thought, and applied the model in various businesses and varying settings, the more the evidence began to mount that the model was valid, and that it worked in applications big and small, simple and complex, and in all sorts of categories and types. With that understanding, the grander possibilities began to emerge, stretching beyond the relationships between brands and their customers. With time, I realized I had a responsibility to do more than just help companies perform better. I was in a position to help companies be and do better in the world. The starkness of that responsibility is similar to Holden Caulfield's self-imposed policing of a field of rye. I, too, desperately want to keep a bunch of kids, the global citizenry, from running off a cliff. It's clear that our choices as global citizens contribute either to our own demise or our own commencement with every single decision we make. Unfortunately, we are marketing, buying, and producing our way into extinction, and there is no referee, parent, or overarching authority, not even the Pope, that can step in and stop us. There is no Holden Caulfield.

It was Tim Draper's commentary—"We need renovation in healthcare, government, and venture capital. That essentially these institutions are no longer viable and need rethought and redone."—that really got me thinking. This idea, that how we are functioning as a global society needs to be refashioned, is increasingly discussed in the mainstream media and among disparate circles of influence throughout the world. Jeremy Rifkin (*The Empathic Civilization*), Sir Richard Branson (The B Team), Arianna Huffington (the Third Metric), Thich Nhat Hanh (the Community of Nations), Ellen MacArthur (the Circular Economy) and Yvon Chouinard (the Responsible Economy) are all concerned with the same issue: there is a disconnect between a vision for the world as a peaceful, sustainable biosphere and our ability to realize that vision as a global society, and as global citizens.

There is, however, this model, this idea, that if we understand truly what makes users and providers tick in every circumstance, then we can design a functioning economy that won't kill us. It's up to us as global citizens to drive the right kind of demand. It's up to the global corporate leadership to use their economic powers for good to design a new, Responsible Economy. It's up to economic policy writers and nation states to design the global economy as it could be. By applying the fundamental tenets of the Brand Ecosystem and the Customer Activation Cycle to any situation where there exists a provider of a service and a user, these three (citizens, corporations, governments) intertwine, and independent entities are capable of living well within the means provided by the planet.

And so, there I stood in the midst of penning this very book with the intention of sharing a decade of learning about how customers come to be avid, committed fans of brands, realizing that the model I was writing about was actually the solution to exactly the disconnect between vision and practice that much of the world's leadership have warned us all about.

Bestselling social critic and economist Jeremy Rifkin summarizes the current state of human consciousness in his book *The Empathic Civilization*, described as follows:

> "Never has the world seemed so completely united—in the form of communication, commerce, and culture—and so savagely torn apart—in the form of war, financial meltdown, global warming, and even the migration of diseases. No matter how much we put our minds to the task of meeting the challenges of a rapidly globalizing world, the human race seems to continually come up short, unable to muster the collective mental resources to truly 'think globally and act locally.'"

This analysis may seem harsh, but considering the pace at which communications have evolved in recent decades, it's understandable that the global populace is just wrapping its collective head around the problems posed by the increased interactions and access to information between citizens of different countries. Nobel Peace Prize nominee Thich Nhat Hanh sees the same challenges from a very different perspective in his treatise the Community of Nations:

> "With the various crises we are witnessing in different parts of the world, it is clear that the era of independent nations with borders and separate interests is gradually coming to a close; that the suffering and pain of one nation is fundamentally linked to and is shared by the hearts of people of all nations; that the instability and depression of another nation effects the prosperity and security of peoples all over the planet. In our present time and place, it is clear that social and economic development and all the challenges that come with it are no longer individual matters. But we are not without hope. The problems that confront our planet and our humanity—environmental tension, social and family dysfunction, economic instability, and political unrest—give us an opportunity to pause, recognize, reexamine the sources of our suffering, and find a path that can lead us toward a brighter future and to an even brighter present."

Thich Nhat Hanh recognized the collapse of previously significant borders, and highlights that we are a global citizenry, newly enriched with the ability to communicate across borders. Yet we still need the means by which to understand one another.

Other influential people in the world are organizing specific efforts to cajole businesses into more responsible behavior. Sir Richard Branson and Jochen Zeitz have launched The B Team, a nonprofit organization of a group of business leaders formed to create a future where the purpose of business is to be the "driving force for social, environmental, and economic benefit." Their mission "is to deliver a Plan B that puts people and planet alongside profit. Plan A—where companies have been driven by the profit motive alone—is no longer acceptable."

The views of how buyers and sellers can coexist sustainably vary, yet overlap. Rifkin sees the solution in refashioning human consciousness "so that human beings can mutually live and flourish in the new globalizing society." Branson and MacArthur believe it is corporate leadership's responsibility to reinvent how we do business and measure success. Chouinard and Badiner (*Mindfulness in the Marketplace*) see the solution as a shared responsibility between providers and consumers, and Thich Nhat Hanh sees the solution residing inside of us as individuals, that through cultivating understanding and compassion, we can develop a greater capacity for empathy, the basis for shared responsibility. The common thread among all of these unique individuals is an attempt to paint a new vision for how we conduct global business and activate sustainable relationships to benefit the biosphere as a whole.

The difficulty for these philosophers, thinkers, and world leaders is that they don't understand, and are not steeped in, the discipline of empirical anthropology, loyalty architecture, or empathic design. Rifkin clearly articulates how far we are from functioning in a harmonious way, in a user experience environment that serves providers and users equally well. It's clear that conceiving of a process to facilitate this experience on a corporate, regional, national, or global scale requires a working model. This then is the challenge: architecting a new way of being, all of us living within the means provided by the planet.

The revelation for me in the chaos of a global environmental crisis is that it is individuals who create demand. Markets respond. It's a common mistake marketing professionals make: thinking that they create demand. They don't. Individuals choose when they have the awareness and means to make a choice. The best marketers can do is present the possibilities. And herein lies the solution to saving the planet: it's going to be good for business to present better possibilities that will ultimately serve our greatest need, an inhabitable planet.

The evidence is mounting that there are three primary areas of concern that threaten the biosphere and require behavioral change on the demand side of the equation, meaning, consumers consuming differently. We as individuals, as a global consuming populace, are driving demand for fossil fuels, water, and agricultural resources in such a way that by the year 2050 (according to the Intergovernmental Panel on Climate Change, IPCC), and some estimate 2035 (according to the International Energy Agency, IEA), life on this planet will change profoundly for the negative.

This excerpt summarizes the risk inherent in these three issues:

> "There are now more than seven billion of us on Earth. As our numbers continue to grow, we continue to increase our need for far more water, far more food, far more land, far more transportation, and far more energy. As a result,

we are now accelerating the rate at which we're changing our climate. In fact, our activities are not only completely interconnected with, but are now also interacting with, the complex system we live on: Earth. It is important to understand how all this is connected."

STEPHEN EMMOTT[xxi]
TEN BILLION

Is this all true, or is it the crazy ramblings of liberal environmentalists? In early 2013, HSBC Bank produced a report for its clientele regarding the long-term value of investments in oil, coal, and natural gas entitled *Oil & Carbon Revisited; Value at Risk from 'Unburnable' Reserves*. The upshot of the report is that HSBC recommends divesting from companies heavily invested in particular oil reserves. Oil seems to have made many a Texan wealthy. Why divert money from oil? The report anticipates a race to realize the value of oil reserves before CO2 emissions overwhelm the planet and global warming reaches the predicted limits that will sustain our existence. They quote the IEA estimating "that in order to have a 50% chance of limiting the rise in global temperatures to two degrees Celsius, only one third of current fossil fuel reserves can be burned before 2050. The balance could be regarded as 'unburnable.'" HSBC believes these reserves will hold no value just thirty-five years from the time this book is published.

If environmentalists are not to be believed, then maybe paying close attention to money is a better indicator of the looming crisis. If not money, then maybe scientists are the ones to pay heed to?

xxi   Stephen Emott, "Humans: the real threat to life on Earth," The Guardian, June 29, 2013. www.theguardian.com/environment/2013/jun/30/stephen-emmott-ten-billion

"Science is essentially organized skepticism. I spend my life trying to prove my work wrong or look for alternative explanations for my results. It's called the Popperian condition of falsifiability. I hope I'm wrong. But the science points to my not being wrong. We can rightly call the situation we're in an unprecedented emergency. We urgently need to do—and I mean actually do—something radical to avert a global catastrophe. But I don't think we will. I think we're fucked. I asked one of the most rational, brightest scientists I know—a scientist working in this area, a young scientist, a scientist in my lab—if there was just one thing he had to do about the situation we face, what would it be? His reply? 'Teach my son how to use a gun.'"

STEPHEN EMMOTT

Milestone steps are being taken by organizations promoting more sustainable practices such as the Sustainable Apparel Coalition (SAC), The B Team, and The Ellen MacArthur Foundation, alongside the efforts of individual companies adhering to the standards evoked in the new B Corporation movement, a new, legal corporate status that redefines success for companies operating "the same as traditional corporations, but with higher standards of corporate purpose, accountability, and transparency."

And there are emerging programs in schools teaching students how to manage the triple bottom line, such as Pepperdine's Graziadio Graduate School of Business' SEER (Social, Environmental, and Ethical Responsibility) program, pioneered by Michael Crooke, PhD.

There are also growing efforts applying pressure for global policy change by grassroots organizations like 350.org and organizations such as the International Energy Agency enacting standards and guidelines for the energy industry as a whole to embrace the challenge.

All of the above assume the responsibility falls on the shoulders of the provider, governments, and regulatory agencies. Of course, without providers assuming the responsibility to initiate the changes necessary, there is certainly no chance our planet survives. However, believing these changes will impact consumer behavior is foolhardy. The vast majority of consumers have little knowledge of the pending doom. Sadly, many don't care. Interviews I personally conducted in the fall of 2013 with a small selection of consumers of a running brand for women revealed an aloof attitude toward corporate sustainability practices in general, and only pragmatic self interest regarding any pending doom:

> "In theory it all sounds good, but it's not going to effect my decision one way or another."

> "I buy workout clothes for workout clothes, I buy my car, a hybrid, because I'm sick of high gas prices, not because it helps the environment."

> "I don't even recycle, it just bugs me."

This is a more stark reality even than the picture Emmott paints. And it underscores his vexation with the status quo. It's not that we should, or could, use the process reviewed in this book to manipulate a customer base to "buy green."

Rather, what I'm suggesting is that through this process we can come to understand the reasons why they don't. We can then reinforce and give authority, depth, complexity, and richness to what might win their attention.

Political, environmental, economic, or spiritual movements tend to rally around what's wrong with the existing system. Downplaying the opposition's position rarely, if ever, motivates a change of mind or heart to a new frame of reference. However, understanding the motivations, needs, concerns, and values of the given constituency is opportunity to find common ground for a relationship. All this is possible through the Brand Ecosystem process.

This unique type and discipline of user experience design is the new imperative for marketers, CEOs, CMOs, VCs, government agencies, and providers of institutionalized services. In Colin Shaw and John Ivens book, *Building Great Customer Experiences*, they cite that 85% of senior business leaders "feel that traditional differentiators alone no longer comprise a sustainable business strategy." And, in addition, that 71% believe that "customer [user] experience is the next corporate battleground."

It is well known that loyal customer behavior is the only thing that truly drives growth and profitability, and guarantees long-term value.

> "...the percentage of customers who were enthusiastic enough to refer a friend or colleague—perhaps the strongest sign of customer

loyalty—correlated directly with differences in growth rates among competitors."

FREDERICK F. REICHHELD[xxii]
HARVARD BUSINESS REVIEW

Architecting the fundamentals that drive loyalty must be the new discipline required in not just the brand creation and development process, but in the process of creating the solutions we speak of here, and specifically are spoken of by Rick Ridgeway in the "Elephant in the Room." In other words, designing and architecting loyalty is the new user experience design imperative that is required to remedy these problems, on both local and global levels. The efficacy of the Customer Activation Cycle has been proven in business. We've learned to apply it at scale. We can now apply this model to design a worldwide economy, an Empathic Civilization, a Circular Economy, in fact, a Responsible Economy.

Remembering Nava Ashraf's abstract, *Rx: Human Nature*, "...[change] requires understanding what makes both end users and providers tick. By understanding the cognitive processes underlying our choices...it's possible to design simple, inexpensive [solutions]." Herein lies the opportunity. Ashraf's work is unearthing solutions to very particular social problems serving as example, a microcosm, of the larger context. The opportunity then, is to expand on this framework by aligning providers and users around a unifying principle that serves not just the needs of the users, but the cognitive processes that motivate and drive their choices. Our mistake as a global

xxii   Frederick F. Reichheld, "The One Number You Need to Grow," *Harvard Business Review*, December 1, 2003. hbr.org/2003/12/the-one-number-you-need-to-grow community has been leaning too heavily on logic and rational thinking to conceive of solutions—solutions in a competitive environment, but also solutions in political, economic, and social settings.

We have lived in the Age of Reason since the late 1700s. We convinced ourselves that we make decisions based on logic. This has created a somewhat lopsided perspective by providers of what users want; i.e., providers typically construct their offers and organizational structure to serve the best interest of the provider while maintaining a competitive service or product offering to the end user or consumer. The capitalistic structure Rick Levine speaks of in *The Cluetrain Manifesto*, measured by profit and driven by the profit motive, is the perfect illustration of this. Levine argued that the Internet would put the marketplace back in the hands of the user, and with that a means to share commonly held beliefs. Some took heed, but most in the corporate world did not, and fewer have taken heed in the arenas of charitable fundraising, social good, education, environmental sustainability, economics, or geo-politics. Few understand that our perception of logical decision-making is a big part of the problem. Kahneman and Tversky have enlightened us that logic is subservient to our true master, intuition. Hence our cognition as users and consumers is driven more by intuition and feel than it is by rational thinking. In fact, taken to its "logical" end, it is our empathic nature that truly drives us. Organizations that are driven by the wrong principles are essentially providing the wrong solutions for the problems we all face today as a global society. As individuals, we are at the mercy of their aftereffects. Daniel Pink, bestselling author of the book *Drive,* concurs that it's not profit motive that drives satisfaction, creativity, or motivation; rather, it's transcendent purpose, autonomy, and mastery that drive us. In Pink's words, "when the profit motive becomes unmoored from the purpose motive, bad things happen; bad things ethically, sometimes, but also bad things like crappy product, lame services, uninspiring places to work. When the profit motive becomes paramount, or becomes completely unhitched from the purpose motive people don't do great things."

Lost in this relationship over time is the intimacy with the end user. With the growth of industry, globalization, and increasing pressures of a wired planet, we lack transparency. We don't know who is behind the curtain pulling the levers and strings that provide products or services. Without this understanding there can be no shared beliefs, no compassion, and no empathy. No empathy means no loyalty. And ultimately, loyalty is the key.

This is how and why Dan Pallotta's business went off the rails, he never established full transparency with his end-users. He never shared his deeply held beliefs about charities and their inability to attract talent and manage money. He never told them his story. Without this platform, his constituency couldn't understand his motivations. They had buckets of compassion ready and waiting to donate to a good cause, but ultimately turned their backs on him and his organization because they didn't have a shared understanding. No empathy begets no loyalty.

Now is the time to work within the cognitive processes at play in the relationship between providers and users and architect solutions based on the expertise and resources of providers, and the specific cognitive processes underlying the needs and motivations of users.

> "The very way our brains are structured disposes us to a way of feeling, thinking, and acting in the world that is no longer entirely relevant to the new environments we have created for ourselves. The human-made environment is rapidly morphing into a global space, yet our existing modes of consciousness are structured for earlier eras of history, which are just as quickly fading away. Humanity finds itself on the cusp of its greatest experiment to date: refashioning human consciousness so that human beings can mutually live and flourish in the new globalizing society..."

JEREMY RIFKIN
THE EMPATHIC CIVILIZATION

The symptoms are everywhere and myriad experts are talking about the problem, but those capable of providing a solution and those identifying the problem are worlds apart. If the solution is a user experience problem, then design is to be the source of the solution, meaning, a new set of user experience criteria is required to yield a positive result. A set of criteria defined by the discipline of user experience design steeped in the understanding of the cognitive processes of both provider and user is needed—the Customer Activation Cycle.

In the summer of 2013, my consulting practice was engaged by an organic vegetable grower to better understand how they could promote their services with the goal of gaining market share for organic produce. Not necessarily gaining market share for their brand in favor of other organic producers, but gaining market share for organics versus commercially grown produce. Their mission was to make organically grown produce available to the masses. They believed in "challenging the status quo in the cause that all may be fed clean food." Their business operated on SEER principles. I built a Customer Activation Cycle for them. Through the process, what we learned by listening to their customers was that at some point these consumers had a significant life event that caused them to explore the health of their immediate ecosystem. The circumstances ranged from the birth of a new baby, to the discovery of a child with a newly formed allergy, or a friend or family member contracting cancer, or something more benign such as a change of heart regarding their own general health and wellbeing. Regardless of the milestone, they attributed the causality of the negative effect somehow to toxicity in their immediate world. They began to connect the dots as they discovered toxins borne in food, water, air, and in the materials that surrounded them, including: cleansers, soaps, shampoos, toothpastes, clothing, bedding, furniture, carpets, paints, automobiles, and even plastic toys. This laundry list isn't compiled overnight. Years pass as the logic extends from one category to the next. It just takes one simple discovery to raise awareness, and then, like the concentric circles emanating from a single drop of water in a quiet pond, understanding extends from their own immediate ecosystem to the biosphere in total. Their behavior follows suit. They begin to clean up their act. Fear of toxicity turns them into rabid activists for their own, and their family's, good, and, finally, as activists for a global solution to the environmental crisis.

Understanding the cognitive processes these users progress through in their personal shift of awareness and behavioral change is achieved by the process of creating the Customer Activation Cycle. This is exactly what I did for this particular client. Strategically, we now understand what is important in these consumers' relationship with this one company. We know the steps necessary to move these users along the Customer Activation Cycle to a point of advocacy. We know the single most important communication about 'clean food' that they need to know to make a first, second, and third purchase. We know how to enlist them in promoting the cause as advocates to their respective circles of influence. We know how and when in their progression to arm them with the materials and information to make demands on their local grocers to carry larger percentages of organic produce versus commercial produce. We know when they are open to hearing that simply shopping at Whole Foods is not enough, that they need to read the labels carefully because not everything at Whole Foods is organic, and until it is, not everyone is safe. We know how to enlist these consumers in support of this company and its mission through their purchases and their advocacy.

This in-depth understanding of resonance between a user and a provider can be understood for any company, system, educational setting, political issue, or even how best to find a common place for users to find motivation in participating in the greening of the planet. I know it sounds idealistic, but driving demand at the point of purchase is our most powerful means to effect change globally, one purchase, one individual, one company, and one system at a time. It's also the proof point to apply this same system to economic policy, national relations, etcetera.

The Dalai Lama said, "If every eight-year-old in the world is taught meditation, we will eliminate violence from the world within one generation." The same is true for saving the planet. The solutions are straightforward: consumers need to stop eating cows, stop having so many babies, stop driving gas-guzzling cars, stop buying useless crap, and shift buying from corporations behaving badly to those measuring their success by more than just profit. The problem is making these issues a high priority within the cognitive processes of the individual consumer in order to create good demand versus bad demand and modify behavior toward conscious consumerism and away from the status quo. As I've said, it's a user experience problem.

In each case, there is a newly defined relationship between the user and the provider. The stuff we are destined to use in the Responsible Economy, the Circular Economy, or in the era of conscious consumerism, is going to require a shift in values and a shift in the perception of ownership and wealth. As example, the Circular Economy is steeped in the concept of Cradle to Cradle manufacturing and distribution.

> "The Circular Economy is a generic term for an economy that is regenerative by design. Materials flows are of two types, biological materials, designed to reenter the biosphere, and technical materials, designed to circulate with minimal loss of quality, in turn entraining the shift toward an economy ultimately powered by renewable energy."
>
> **WORLD ECONOMIC FORUM**
> *TOWARDS THE CIRCULAR ECONOMY*

Manufacturers in this instance no longer think of their business in terms of unit sales, rather they think in terms of delivering an end service by providing a long-lasting, upgradable, durable product. Users in this relationship obtain these 'services' by leasing rather than buying outright. A prime example is of a rentable laundry washing machine. The manufacturer provides the machine for a fee for a set number of loads. When the machine reaches a predetermined number of loads it would be replaced by a new machine, the old machine going back to the manufacturer for an upgrade path in preparation to be "rented" again. Any parts discarded would be recycled. Parts that were still serviceable would go back into the field. Users get a quality product in perpetuity. In effect, there are myriad other forms of thought surrounding the Circular Economy, such as materials that become resources for another process once they've served their useful life in an original application. The general idea is that all things are essentially temporary, as in nature, and the waste of one thing becomes a life resource for another thing. In our culture of ownership, status, and value associated with the accumulation of material things, the Circular Economy has a significant cultural cognitive limitation to overcome. From what is known about loyalty and the Customer Activation Cycle, these cognitive processes can be known and a new alignment of values established such that the tenets of the Circular Economy can be adopted more seamlessly by the masses rather than an elite few.

Companies adopting these practices need to understand the profitability they seek is a function of the loyalty they receive; and, that with a new awareness developed among consumers comes a new wave of demand that will drive the change required to stave off what is currently the inevitable. Very much akin to the example I witnessed among organic tomato buyers, their change of buying habits occurred through increased awareness of the impact environmental toxins had on their immediate family. The evolution of lifestyle and buying habits of these people were not motivated by political agendas, economics, social consciousness, environmental activism, or marketing. They were motivated by the love of their families. Buying organic tomatoes was just one tiny result, but a small step led to many more steps in a shift to more conscious consumption.

What we know is that long-term, sustainable loyalty is most sticky in ethical businesses. The brand bond is greatest with B Corporation businesses. We also know that cheerleaders advocate for the ethical purposes and drive these organizations. If we are to scale a movement on the demand side with consumers, raising their awareness and inspiring them to make better choices as consumers, it becomes the responsibility of these organizations to promote the value of their particular approaches to audiences in such a way that it shifts their awareness, expands their knowledge, and informs them. This is transparency that extends well beyond the profit motive. It's time for green businesses to stop preaching to the choir, and it's time for non-green businesses to realize that there is vast opportunity in doing the right thing. It's time for both camps to engage in exposing large numbers of people, the global citizenry, to their power in this equation. The means to do so, the means to understand the cognitive processes of potential users of any service, is via the Customer (or Global Citizen) Activation Cycle.

In the case of the Responsible Economy and conscious consumerism, there is again a cultural value proposition that it is required to overcome. In this instance, it is more in the communication of the value of the products being produced. As example, the Sustainable Apparel Coalition (SAC), founded in 2009, has established a tool for measuring the environmental and social performance of apparel products.

> "The Sustainable Apparel Coalition was founded by a group of sustainability leaders from global apparel and footwear companies who recognize that addressing our industry's current social and environmental challenges are both a business imperative and an opportunity. Through multi-stakeholder engagement, the Coalition seeks to lead the industry toward a shared vision of sustainability built upon a common approach for measuring and evaluating apparel and footwear product sustainability performance that will spotlight priorities for action and opportunities for technological innovation."

The tool is known as the Higg Index and is at the root of providing a means to understand the relative impact across the life cycle of a product, including its materials, manufacturing, packaging, transportation, use, and end-of-life. An invaluable endeavor already adopted in 2013 by companies responsible for more than a third of the clothing and footwear produced on the planet.

In the global marketplace, this means that consumers have choice. Consumers can participate in the reduction of the negative impact of manufacturing simply through their purchases from companies participating and realizing the standard being put in place by the SAC. The crux of the matter, however, is the current limited demand for environmentally conscious product.

Bill McKibbon's "350" movement is a grassroots movement to solve the climate crisis, now with thousands of volunteer organizers in 188 countries. Certified B Corporations are "a global movement to redefine success in business," with a growing membership of more than 1,000 companies in thirty-three countries. These are examples of just two organizations purposefully pursuing tangible change. In the scheme of things, these are relatively small numbers on a planet with a population of seven billion and growing.

In order to effect the change required at scale, we need to understand quite simply the beliefs and motivations of all people in order to craft the Empathic Civilization to which Jeremy Rifkin alludes.

As we move into an entirely new realm of realities thrust upon us by a burgeoning global population and the costs of rampant consumerism, it's easy to convince ourselves someone is going to come along and save the day, that technology will rescue us, or that somehow the governing bodies of the world's super powers will devise a policy change that will eradicate the ruin. The truth is, the change required is all of our responsibility. There actually is latent demand for good product that does less harm. Marketers, business owners, and leaders need to learn how to understand the connective tissue between this latent demand and how they have learned to communicate value. Consumers need choice, and business people need to understand there is profit in not doing business as usual.

There's no time left for business as usual.

Understanding Advocacy: Defined Terms

PROGRESSION OF RESONANCE
CUSTOMER ACTIVATION CYCLE
STORY UNIVERSE
RATE OF MIGRATION
FIVE BONDS OF LOYALTY
BRAND ECOSYSTEM

Understanding how resonance happens, the connection between us, is the foundation to understanding how to engender a following. It is the key to how relationships form: a relationship between two people, a company and a customer, or an organization and its constituents. Every human relationship happens in simple steps. A first impression leads to validation of that first impression, which leads to deeper understanding and an alignment of beliefs: blink, test, bond, love. We move from a superficial introduction to a deep state of resonance. This is how loyalty works. It's a **Progression of Resonance** (see page 61).

Architecting loyalty is possible in any circumstance. It requires understanding how resonance happens, understanding both the provider of a service and the user of that service. Alignment of needs becomes alignment of beliefs, a meeting of the minds, the provider not only meeting expectations but also communicating why it meets those expectations in the particular ways that it does. "Different strokes for different folks" was never more relevant than in the case of a brand providing a service or goods to a customer. Just like the resonance in relationships between people, customers move along a progression from first impression to deep understanding. Along that path, the customer transcends mere loyalty and can become an advocate for the brand, its beliefs, and its services. It's how customers say I love you, through their advocacy, and it ultimately leads to greater sales velocity and sustainable growth. The model that allows us to understand, enact, and measure a brand's ability to create advocacy is the **Customer Activation Cycle** (see page 52).

Understanding why resonance (advocacy, love) happens and how it happens is only part of the process of architecting a following. Deep resonance happens vis-à-vis milestone experiences and stories—stories and experiences that exist as expressions of the unique reason why the organization exists, its raison d'etre. Being certain that at any moment, in any instance, the core reason for being is manifest in every single communication and experience is the only way to guarantee that deep understanding will ultimately happen. If it doesn't happen, the relationship will falter and one party will fall away from the other. If the core value held by the organization is present in every seemingly trivial interaction with the user, if a conviction of belief is present in every nuance and moment, then the provider and user are destined to agree or disagree. Agreement means resonance. Mapping the stories and milestone experiences that lead to advocacy is the means by which any provider of a service or product can guarantee that its reason for being is manifest in every interaction with the end user. This is the **Story Universe** (see pages 50 and 51).

Together, these three models, or tools, form the Brand Ecosystem, and are the means to architecting meaningful relationships between providers and users. These are functional tools for migrating a potential user of any product or service to a point of advocacy. The Brand Ecosystem holistically describes how indifference morphs into enthusiasm, how apathy turns into action, how causes rally support, and how brands build rabid, long-term loyalty. The revolutionary perspective that separates this thinking from all other brand relationship management theory is the Activation Cycle seen as a fractal (see page 109).

When considering this, we can describe customers constantly being in the process of becoming a long-term sustainable customer. The customer may not be activating to the next stage, they could be moving back to a more nascent stage, which is fine (destined to remain casuals, loyalists, or even prospects because they don't align with the first impression or any of the values within the progression). To migrate to the next stage, they simply have to reenter the process of **Migration** (see pages 107 and 108). If they continue to progress, that's accounted for in the quantitative metrics of migration. If they don't, it provides the opportunity to understand why, what is missing in the experiences or communications that dissatisfy that particular individual. If there is a remedy and it can be enacted, then that customer is afforded the opportunity to reenter the fray and continue along the migration. This is not a case of chasing customers that fundamentally disagree, these customers are truly destined to become lost souls and not demonstrate any loyalty now or in the future; rather, viewing the **Customer Activation Cycle** as a fractal is a means by which the organization can understand fully it's ability to provide an aligned user experience for customers that do agree with the brand's point of view every step along the path to advocacy.

As the value provided by a brand becomes aligned with the core needs of the customer, the greater the importance that brand plays in the individual's life. Purpose moves from utilitarian to transcendent, and customers become advocates—because it's good for them. Brands provide a value beyond just product quality and experience. That value might be as simple as convenience or as lofty as an ethical belief.

In the end, it is ethical purpose where true loyalty resides. Customers believe their association with ethical companies is something that makes their world a little bit better, and in so doing, the company creates satisfaction and motivates them to take action. It turns out we customers want to be part of something bigger than ourselves. Something that will help us achieve something that we can't necessarily achieve on our own. When we find a company that believes in what we believe, we form a near-unbreakable bond. The **Five Bonds of Loyalty** (see page 142) helps visualize the intensity of bonds based on this spectrum from utility to belief.

Taking this macro view of loyalty demonstrates how important it is for providers of goods and services to understand the **Progression of Resonance** and to craft their own **Brand Ecosystem** as a means to assure sustainable, long-term relationships with their constituency.

Index

Symbols

350.org 213

A

Abercrombie & Fitch 167
A/B testing 17, 105
actualized brand relationship 126
Adidas 144
Adility 137
Adobe 17, 47
Advertising for Humanity 31
Affinity Ladder 188
Age of Reason 216
AIDS Rides 31
Albert, Einstein 12
Alfa Romeo 158
All Marketers Are Liars 86
Amazon 18, 135, 137, 139, 151, 153
  Amazon Prime 151
America 151
American Apparel 167, 168
American Management Association 92
Anderson, Ray 168
Apple 40, 45, 119, 121, 135, 136, 169
Arneson, Hal 177, 179
Ashraf, Nava 25, 26, 215

B

Badiner, Allan Hunt 11, 209
Bain & Company 91
Bakersfield 7
Barnes & Noble 134, 135, 136
B Corp 169, 212, 223, 225
Begley's Best 123
Behavioral Loyalty 77

Bergstrom, Corey 106, 107
Bering Strait 181
Big Data 105, 106
Bizzarrini 159
Black Angus 140
Blockbuster 151, 152
Bloomberg News 138
BMW 131, 132, 133, 134, 160, 161
Bohm, David 128, 148
BP 2
Brand Advocates 90, 91
brand bond 149
Brand Ecosystem 4, 12, 18, 19, 39, 41, 47, 77, 173, 200,
        206, 214
Branson, Richard 11, 206, 208, 209
Braungart, Michael 11
Breast Cancer 3-Day 31
Breen, Bill 123
B Team, The 11, 206, 208, 212
Buddhism 79
Building Great Customer Experiences 214
Business News Daily 91

C

Cabela's 105, 106, 107, 108, 109, 110, 116, 117, 118, 124
California 6, 67, 74, 140
Catcher in the Rye, The 204
Caulfield, Holden 205, 206
Central Valley 6, 7, 8
Cervelo Bicycles 158
Channel Islands 79
Charity Case 32
Cheers 163
Cheese Board Collective 2
Chiat Day 169
Chouinard, Yvon 3, 8, 9, 10, 43, 99, 206, 209
Chris on Cars 158
Circular Economy 11, 13, 206, 221, 222

Clark, Kim 75, 84
Clark, Kurt 97
clean climbing 8, 9
climbing Mount Sustainability 168
Cloudveil 16, 119
Cluetrain Manifesto, The 34, 216
Coca-Cola 10, 149, 155, 156, 157
cognitive basis for human errors 102
Coke 154
Columbia 16
Community of Nations 206, 208
company principles 62, 69
conscious consumerism 221, 224
core user 104, 190
core value 52, 57, 58, 66, 68, 69, 73, 74, 86, 89, 140, 166,
        191, 228
Cradle to Cradle: Remaking the Way We Make Things 11,
        221
Critique of Pure Reason 20
Crooke, Michael 84, 87, 212
Cubs, The 163
Customer Activation Cycle 41, 48, 49, 53, 56, 57, 58, 59,
        60, 61, 65, 72, 88, 89, 111, 116, 118, 120, 121, 122,
        125, 126, 127, 173, 174, 184, 194, 200, 201, 206, 215,
        218, 219, 220, 222, 224, 228, 230
    casual 57, 58, 61, 66, 67, 69, 72, 73, 84, 104, 110, 114,
        118, 119, 126, 166, 190, 191, 229
    cheerleader 58, 60, 61, 62, 68, 69, 72, 73, 75, 90, 104,
        110, 111, 114, 115, 118, 119, 120, 121, 127, 129, 185,
        186, 191, 194, 223
    lost soul 113, 117, 230
    loyalist 58, 61, 67, 68, 69, 72, 73, 104, 110, 114, 118, 119,
        126, 191, 229
    model 104, 109, 117
    prospect 57, 58, 61, 66, 67, 69, 72, 73, 104, 118, 119, 121,
        127, 190, 194, 229
customer profitability management 112
Customer Relationship Management 17, 47, 48, 49, 108,
        111, 112, 113, 122

D

Dalai Lama, The 221
Dells 119
Del Vecchio, Gene 147
Denmark 35
DiGo Brands 90
Dino 142
dirtbag 81
dog walker 96, 147
Dow Chemical 2
Draper, Tim 5, 206
Drive 77, 86, 217

E

Ecover 123
Eddie Bauer 97, 98, 101, 104, 129, 133, 170
Edison, Thomas 46
Einstein, Albert 100
Elephant in the Room, The 5, 10, 215
Ellen MacArthur Foundation, The 212
Emerson, Daniel 75
Emmott, Stephen 211, 212, 213
Empathic Civilization, The 206, 207
Enterprise Rent-a-Car 48

F

Facebook 175
Fast Company 123
Fat Tire Ale 2
Ferrari 129, 141, 142, 143, 158, 159, 160
Ferrari, Enzo 142, 143, 158, 159, 160
Fischer, Martin H. 172
Five Bonds of Loyalty 150, 151, 154, 230
    caveat 52, 151, 155, 160, 163, 167, 186
    confusion and clarity 151, 152, 156, 160, 164, 168
    convenience 18, 151, 152, 153, 230
    ethical 156, 166, 167, 168, 169, 191, 223, 230

prime takeaway 151, 153, 157, 162, 165, 169
promotional 16, 123, 138, 140, 154, 156, 157
superior 63, 157, 161, 162
tribal 8, 156, 162, 165, 191
winners and losers 151, 153, 156, 161, 165, 168
Flor 168
Ford, Henry 46
Forrester Research 129, 135
Frost, Tom 9
Fruit Loops 2

G

Gartner Inc. 111
General Mills 98
General Motors 161
Gladwell, Malcolm 96
Godin, Seth 86, 121, 122
Goldstein, Lee 90
Grand Tourers 159
Groupon 136, 137, 138, 139

H

Hanh, Thich Nhat 3, 206, 207, 208, 209
Harley Davidson 40, 162, 163, 164
Harvard 32, 180
Harvard Business Review 48, 215
Heart of the Buddha's Teaching, The 3
Hewlett-Packard 10
Higg Index, The 224
Holifield, David 150
HomeRun 137
HSBC Bank 211
Huffington, Arianna 206

I

IBM 17, 47, 49, 64
Integrated Design Engineering 66
INTERFuel 150

Intergovernmental Panel on Climate Change 210
International Energy Agency 210, 211, 213
iPad 135
Isigonis, Alec 132, 134
Ivens, John 214
Iwata, Jon 64, 84

J

J. Crew 167
Jedidiah 167
Jobs, Steve 30, 31, 41, 46, 169
Jolt Cola 156, 157
Jones Soda 155, 156

K

Kahneman, Daniel 19, 102, 103, 110, 216
Kant, Immanuel 14, 20
Key Performance Metrics 48
Kindle 135
King Jr., Martin Luther 30, 31

L

Lakers, The 162
Lamborghini 158, 159, 160
Lamborghini, Ferruccio 158, 160
Lancia 158
Lefkosky, Eric 137, 138
Levine, Rick 34, 216
Levi's 167
Light & Motion 66, 67, 68, 69, 72, 73, 74, 75
Lincoln, Abraham 38
Linda Problem, The 102, 103, 104, 105, 106, 110, 119
Living Social 137
Los Angeles 140
loyalty architect 15
Loyalty Effect: The Hidden Force Behind Growth, The
       91, 105
Loyalty Ladder 189

Lululemon 125, 153
luxe populi 123

M

MacArthur, Ellen 11, 206, 209
MacMillan, Douglas 138
Madison Avenue 34
Marina 67
Mason, Andrew 136, 137
Maturana, Humberto R. 23
McDonald's 35
McDonough, William 11
McKibbon, Bill 225
McLeod, Saul 21
McQuivey, James 135
Mercedes 158, 161
Mercedes Benz 160, 161
Method 123
Mexico 79
Microsoft 47
Mies van der Rohe, Ludwig 50
Mindfulness in the Marketplace 11, 209
MINI 131, 132, 133, 146
  Cooper 132
  Coupe 133
MIT Sloan Management Review 116
Miura 158
Mountain Hardware 16
Muhammad Ali 144

N

National Geographic 178
National Public Radio 5
Native Foods 139, 140
natural frequency 16, 45, 63
Naturopathica 185, 187
Nau 165
Netflix 18, 152

Net Promoter Index 48, 50, 51
Nielsen, Jacob 20
Nike 147
Nin, Anaïs 19
Noma's 35
Nook 134, 135
· North America 106

O

Oil & Carbon Revisited 211
Orange County 140
Oreos 147
organizing principle 42, 45, 47, 82

P

Pallotta, Dan 31, 32, 33, 217
Patagonia 3, 4, 6, 8, 9, 10, 11, 16, 34, 35, 40, 42, 43, 44, 45,
        80, 81, 82, 83, 84, 87, 89, 98, 99, 119, 120, 129, 130,
        145, 164, 165, 176, 177, 179, 180, 181, 182, 183, 243
    Capilene 181
    Cotton Tour 5, 6, 7
Pepperdine's Graziadio Graduate School of Business 212
Pepsi 149, 154, 155, 156, 157
Perceptual Set, The 21, 23
Pink, Daniel 77, 78, 83, 86, 216, 217
Point, The 136, 137
Porsche 75, 132
prAna 124, 125, 126, 153
principles of company, product, and service 73
Prius 158
Progression of Resonance 27, 65, 227, 230
    blink 64, 121, 122, 131, 190, 192, 227
    bond 64, 121, 122, 131, 190, 191, 192, 227
    love 64, 121, 122, 131, 190, 191, 192, 227
    test 64, 121, 122, 131, 190, 191, 192, 227

R

Rate of Migration 48, 61, 105, 108, 110, 111, 115, 120,
        126, 193

Red Bull 156
Reichheld, Frederick F. 91, 105, 215
Responsible Company, The 3
Responsible Economy, The 5, 11, 206, 224
Ridgeway, Rick 10, 12, 215
Rifkin, Jeremy 206, 207, 209, 218, 225
Road & Track 133
Robinson, Doug 9
Rodway, Julie 98
RX: Human Nature: How Behavioral Economics Is Pro-
       moting Better Health Around the World Harvard
       Business School 26, 215

S

Saint-Exupery, Antoine de 42
Salesforce 47
Salinger, J. D. 204
SAS Institute 106
Scoop 137
Scott, Walter 16
Seattle Post-Intelligencer 97
SEER 169, 212, 219
Seventh Generation 123, 164
Shaw, Colin 214
Signal and the Noise, The 76
Silicon Valley 1
Silver, Nate 76
Sinek's Golden Circle 30
Sinek, Simon 29, 30, 50, 96
Skype 158
Southern California 139
Southwest 147
Stanford's Graduate School of Business 103
Stanley, Vincent 3
Start With Why 29, 96
Stella 300 Dual headlights 73
Story Universe 41, 48, 49, 52, 53, 54, 59, 60, 65, 69, 72, 73,
       74, 75, 88, 89, 173, 194, 195, 196, 197, 200, 229

strategy
  Blue Ocean 170
  Cost 170
  Differentiation 170
  Focus 170
  Innovation 170
  Red Ocean 155, 170
  Technology 170
Super Bowl 146
Surfers Journal 178
Sustainable Apparel Coalition 212, 224, 225
Swoop 137

T

Teal, Thomas 105
Technology Review 107
TED 31, 33
Ten Billion 211
Tesla 158
The Kernel 93, 94, 101, 104
  core users 94, 96, 97, 98, 101, 174
  dog walkers 95, 96, 97, 98, 99, 101
  founding vision 93, 94, 98
The North Face 16, 34, 35
Thinking, Fast and Slow 102
Third Metric 206
Tiger 75
Tipping Point, The 96, 102
Toyota 145, 158, 161
Tree of Knowledge, The 23
TripAdvisor 175
Tversky, Amos 19, 102, 110, 216

U

Under One Roof 66, 67
United States 6, 9
University of California, Irvine 79
usability testing 17

V

Value at Risk from 'Unburnable' Reserves 211
Vancouver 153
Varela, Francisco 23
Ventura 6, 8
Vision Statement 87, 88
Volvo 160, 161
VW Beetle 132

W

Wall Street 5
Walmart 2, 10, 18
Watts, Alan 79, 81
Way We Think About Charity is Dead Wrong, The 31
West, Cornel 28
Whole Foods Market 87, 88, 89, 220
Whole Natural Art of Protection, The 9
Windows 169
Wired 32
World Series 163

X

Xbox 31

Y

Yelp 175
YouTube 66

Z

Zambia 25
Zappos 152, 153
Zeitz, Jochen 11, 208

Acknowledgments

There are just a handful of people throughout my life that have had lasting impact on my values and thinking. Yvon Chouinard is one of them. I count myself lucky to have spent some time inside the company he founded and was blessed to be eyewitness to his beliefs manifest in daily actions. I'll be forever grateful for the perspective and lessons of integrity learned. Along with YC, there are a number of other people that shaped my work during and after my days at Patagonia. They include: Rick Ridgeway, Hal Arneson, Morlee Griswold, Chris Todd, Bill Boland, Jason Bowman, David Holifield, Jeff Wogoman, Matt Levinthal, Perry Klebahn, and Rich Hill. I'd be remiss if I didn't thank Michael Crooke, PhD (former CEO, Patagonia) specifically for spearheading Patagonia's multichannel strategies during my tenure.

I've also been remarkably lucky to count some very smart business leaders and entrepreneurs as my clients, many who've shaped this work by challenging its assumptions and demanding pragmatism so that the ideas function in the real world and not just in theory. I'd like to especially thank Scott Kerslake (CEO, prAna Living), Daniel Emerson (CEO, Light & Motion), Rich Hill (VP sales prAna Living, CEO Ibex, Founder Ticla), Keith Anderson (VP of marketing, Ibex), and Ricardo Crisantes (GM, Wholesum Family Farms).

I'm overwhelmingly grateful for the team that collaborated to create the book. I had no idea how large the contribution was to be across the spectrum of talent that ultimately produced the book. Kate Sage, tutor as much as editor, shepherded the text from a collection of disparate ideas into a cogent capture of the work. Stratton Cherouny oversaw the entirety of the look and feel, including finding Jeremy Collins and convincing him it would be time well spent off the mountain and out of the editing room to pen the illustrations. And Tyson Cornell and Rare Bird Books for taking a chance on publishing a first time author and seeing that every detail came together in its best form. Thank you doesn't begin to express my appreciation for the collective effort.

A couple final thank-you's. Patrick Callahan, who contributed his time and energy not just convincing me to write, but handholding me through the beginning stages of the manuscript. If not for Patrick I never would have embarked. And, most importantly, to my wife Tracy Hulett. I'm not certain how best to articulate my gratitude for my lifelong partner in life, parenting, and business who has been a willing participant in our roller coaster entrepreneurial adventures questioning the status quo. For two years she's read, edited, encouraged, and collaborated as I've worked through every fit and start. I'm forever grateful for her keeping me, and us, afloat in body, mind and spirit.

With gratitude,
cw